EXCEL Statistics

EXCEL Statistics

A Quick Guide

Neil J. Salkind

University of Kansas

Los Angeles | London | New Delhi
Singapore | Washington DC

For information:

SAGE Publications, Inc.
2455 Teller Road
Thousand Oaks, California 91320
E-mail: order@sagepub.com

SAGE Publications Ltd.
1 Oliver's Yard
55 City Road
London EC1Y 1SP
United Kingdom

SAGE Publications India Pvt. Ltd.
B 1/I 1 Mohan Cooperative
Industrial Area
Mathura Road, New Delhi 110 044
India

SAGE Publications Asia-Pacific Pte. Ltd.
33 Pekin Street #02-01
Far East Square
Singapore 048763

Printed in the United States of America

Library of Congress Cataloging-in-Publication Data

Excel statistics : a quick guide / Neil J. Salkind.
p. cm.
Includes bibliographical references and index.
ISBN 978-1-4129-7963-4 (pbk.)
1. Microsoft Excel (Computer file) 2. Social sciences--Statistical methods–Computer programs. 3. Electronic spreadsheets. I. Salkind, Neil J.

HF5548.4.M523E95 2011
005.54—dc22 2010013967

This book is printed on acid-free paper.

10 11 12 13 14 10 9 8 7 6 5 4 3 2 1

Acquisitions Editor: Vicki Knight
Associate Editor: Lauren Habib
Editorial Assistant: Ashley Dodd
Production Editor: Libby Larson
Copy Editor: Liann Lech
Typesetter: C&M Digitals (P) Ltd.
Proofreader: Theresa Kay
Indexer: Terri Corry
Cover Designer: Candice Harman
Marketing Manager: Stephanie Adams

Contents

How to Use This Book

Who *Excel Statistics: A Quick Guide* Is For . . .

Excel Statistics: A Quick Guide is about how to use the functions and Analysis ToolPak available in Excel 2010. It was written for several general audiences.

For those enrolled in introductory statistics courses, *Excel Statistics: A Quick Guide* provides experience with the world's most popular spreadsheet program, Excel, and how its features can be used to answer both simple and complex questions about data. *Excel Statistics: A Quick Guide* can also serve as an ancillary text to help students understand how an application such as Excel complements the introductory study of statistics.

For those who are more familiar with statistics, perhaps students in their second course or social or behavioral scientists or business researchers, *Excel Statistics: A Quick Guide* can be used to concisely show how functions and Analysis ToolPak tools can be used in applied situations. These users might consider *Excel Statistics: A Quick Guide* as a reference book where they can pick and choose what it is they need to learn to do and move on to different functions or tools as they need to learn how and when to use them.

Excel Statistics: A Quick Guide does not teach the reader how to use Excel as a spreadsheet application. It is assumed that the user of the book has some familiarity with basic computer operations (such as clicking and dragging) and also has some knowledge of how to use Excel (such as entering and editing data and saving files). Should you desire an introductory book that combines both the basics of statistics plus the use of Excel (beyond what is offered here), then you might want to look at Salkind's *Statistics for People Who (Think They) Hate Statistics (Excel Edition),* also published by SAGE.

How to Use *Excel Statistics: A Quick Guide*

Excel Statistics: A Quick Guide is designed in a very special way.

Each of the 30 functions in Part 1 covers a 2-page spread. On the left-hand side of the page is text and on the right-hand side of the page are the figures (two per QuickGuide) that illustrate the ideas introduced in the text. This design and this format allow the user to see what the use of the Excel function looks like as it is being applied. It's easy to go from the text to the illustrations and back again if necessary.

Each of the 15 Analysis ToolPak tools in Part 2 also uses a 2-page spread as well and two figures, except that sometimes, one of the figures appears on the left-hand page along with the text. This is because much of the resulting output takes up a considerable amount of physical page space and simply needs more room to be fully appreciated and understood.

With the above in mind, please note the following:

- If you are new to functions or the Analysis ToolPak, spend some time reading the introductions to Part 1 and Part 2 on pages 1 and 69. They will get you started quickly as to how to use these Excel features.
- If you are familiar with functions and the Analysis ToolPak, then start looking through the functions and tools to get an idea of what is considered and how the material is organized.
- Each of the functions and tools is accompanied by an Excel file that is used as an example in the analyses that are presented. These files are available in two places: the SAGE Web site at (www.sagepub.com/salkind excelstats), and the author's personal Web site at www.onlinefile folder.com. Look for the Excel QG folder. The username is *ancillaries* and the password is *files.* Please contact me at njs@ku.edu should you have any difficulty downloading these and I will send them to you immediately.
- *Excel Statistics: A Quick Guide* is as much a reference book as anything else, and you should feel free to experiment with the use of functions and tools that serve the same general purpose (such as the CORREL function and the Correlation ToolPak tool) and use all of Excel's very powerful features. For example, much of the output you see in *Excel Statistics: A Quick Guide* has been reformatted to better fit the page and look more attractive. This can be accomplished easily through the use of built-in Excel features such as table formatting. Excel is a very flexible tool, and you can use the output you generate through functions or through the use of tools in many different ways and in many different settings.

About the Windows and Macintosh Versions

The latest Windows and Macintosh versions of Excel are identical in many ways. The screens' appearance may appear just a bit different, but that is as much a function of the operating system as it is of the Excel application. And, there are clear (but minor) differences between the two in how you navigate around an Excel window and how you perform certain types of operations. For example, in Windows you can copy a cell's contents by using the Ctrl + C key combination, whereas with the Mac, you use the Command ⌘ (Apple) + C key combination. Anyone familiar with either operating system will understand these differences and you can feel comfortable using either version of the program. Once you know how to use the basics of Excel, the learning curve for the other version is not very steep.

However, the two versions do differ in some significant ways.

As far as functions go, the Mac version uses a very simple and efficient Formula Builder to construct formulas and use functions. However, a significant disadvantage of the Mac version is that there is no Analysis ToolPak. If you want to do a more advanced analysis like the ones we illustrate in Part II of *Excel Statistics: A Quick Guide,* then download StatPlus:mac LE (for free from AnalystSoft), which was available at this writing, and then use StatPlus:mac LE with Excel 2008.

Also, every few years, Microsoft, the developer of Excel, releases a new version of Excel. Usually, these new versions offer new and additional features, and just as often, many existing features stay the same. For the most part, the functions that you see in these pages work the same way as the functions in Microsoft 97–2003 and even Excel 5.0/95. So, although the images in these pages and the described steps are accurate and were developed using Excel 2010, you should have no concerns that these QuickGuides will not work with your version of Excel. Also, with the introduction of Excel 2010, Microsoft added some variants of formulas designed only for use with 2010. However, there are corresponding functions and Analysis ToolPak tools that will work with any version, and those are the ones that we cover.

A Note to the Instructor

We have developed a chart that is available at www.onlinefilefolder.com (look in the Excel QG folder) that shows the corresponding coverage with the coverage of a variety of introductory textbooks. We hope that helps you in your teaching and better prepares you to include this material as part of the coursework. If you use another book and want that information added to the chart, please let me know at njs@ku.edu.

Acknowledgments

There are always many people to thank when a book comes to fruition, and let me first thank Vicki Knight, senior editor at SAGE, for her editorship, guidance, patience, and willingness to talk through lots of aspects of the project. Thanks also to Lisa Shaw for the same willingness to listen and help out. Others to thank are Libby Larson for making this book look as good as it does (even if the author had a few crazy comments), Ashley Dodd and Lauren Habib for making sure things got to where they needed to get to on time, and, as always, Liann Lech, the best copy editor (and teacher) in the galaxy. Want to know when you should use *because* and when you should use *since*? Ask me. Now I know. And, thanks to all the people at SAGE who seem to care as much about their authors as what their authors write.

And this book is for Russ Shafer-Landau, major foodie and a friend without equal.

Corrections? Ideas? Concerns? Anything—let me know. Thanks.

Neil J. Salkind
njs@ku.edu

About the Author

Neil J. Salkind received his PhD from the University of Maryland in Human Development and taught at the University of Kansas for 35 years, where he is now professor emeritus. He has written more than 125 professional papers and presentations, and he is the author of several college-level textbooks, including *Statistics for People Who (Think They) Hate Statistics* (SAGE), *Theories of Human Development* (SAGE), *Exploring Research* (Prentice Hall), and the *Encyclopedia of Measurement and Statistics* (SAGE). Other SAGE texts by Salkind can be found at www.sagepub.com/salkind. He was the editor of *Child Development Abstracts and Bibliography* for 13 years and lives in Lawrence, Kansas, where he likes to read, swim with the River City Sharks, bake brownies (see the Excel version of *Statistics for People . . .* for the recipe), and poke around old Volvos and old houses.

PART I

USING EXCEL FUNCTIONS

A function is a formula that is predefined to accomplish a certain task. *Excel Statistics: A Quick Guide* deals with those tasks that are statistical in nature, and in this introduction, we will show the general steps for using any Excel function.

Although there are many different types of functions (such as AVERAGE and STDEV) in many different categories (such as financial, logical, and engineering), we will be dealing only with those that focus on working with numerical data and performing elementary and advanced operations—in other words, those that fall in the group of functions known as *statistical.*

A Simple Example

In Figure A1, you can see a column of 10 numbers, with the average appearing in Cell B11. Take a look at the formula bar at the top of the figure and you will see the syntax for this function. Like this . . .

=AVERAGE(B1:B10)

Figure A1 A Simple Function That Computes the Average of a Set of Values

B11 | =AVERAGE(B1:B10)

function [Compatibility Mode]

	A	B	C	D	E
1		2			
2		2			
3		5			
4		7			
5		5			
6		6			
7		3			
8		6			
9		5			
10		4			
11	Average	4.5			

Some general things to remember about using functions:

1. Functions always begin with an equal (=) sign as the first character entered in a cell.

2. A function can be placed in any cell. It will return the value of that function in that cell. It often makes the most sense to place the function near the data you are describing.

3. As you can see in Figure A1, the syntax of the function [located in the formula bar, which is =AVERAGE(B1:B10)] is not what is returned to the cell, but rather the *value* computed by the function (in this case, 4.5).

4. A function can be entered manually by typing in the syntax and the range (or ranges of cells that are to be applied), or it can be entered automatically. We'll review both methods in this introduction, but *Excel Statistics: A Quick Guide* will focus exclusively on the automatic

method because it is easier and faster, and it can always be edited manually if necessary.

The Anatomy of a Function

Let's take a quick look at what makes up a function, and then we will move on to how to enter one.

Here's the function that you saw earlier in Figure A1 that computes the average for a range of scores:

=AVERAGE(B1:B10)

And, here is what each element represents . . .

Function Element	*What It Does*
=	Functions always start with an equal sign.
AVERAGE	The name of the function.
(B1:B10)	The range of cells to which the function will be applied. Ranges always appear in parentheses.

Entering a Function Manually

To enter an Excel function manually, you have to know two things:

1. The name of the function.
2. The syntax or structure of the function. You can see by the example that we have been using that AVERAGE is the name of the function and the syntax is

=AVERAGE(range of cells)

Some functions are simple and others are quite complex. You can find out the names of all available Excel functions, what they do, and the associated syntax through Excel Help.

Entering a Function Automatically

This is by far the fastest and easiest method and will be the model that will be used throughout *Excel Statistics: A Quick Guide.* You still have to know what function you need to use.

1. Click on the cell where you want the function to be placed. In the example we are using here, the cell is B11.

2. Click Formulas → Insert Function and you will see the Insert Function dialog box as shown in Figure A2.

Figure A2 The Insert Function Dialog Box

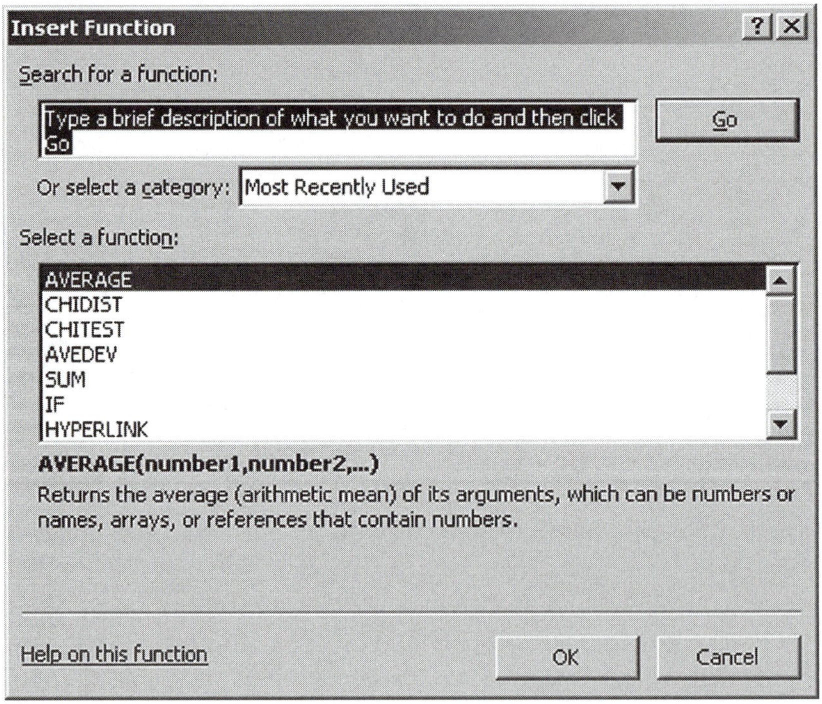

3. Locate the function you want to use by using the Search for a function: box and the Go button, selecting a category and a function, or selecting a function from the list that shows the most recently used functions. In our example, AVERAGE is the function of interest.

4. Double-click on the AVERAGE function in the list (or any other function) and you will see the all-important Function Arguments Box shown in Figure A3.

Figure A3 The Function Arguments Dialog Box for the AVERAGE function

Function Arguments
AVERAGE
Number1 B1:B10 = {2;2;5;7;5;6;3;6;5;4}
Number2 = number
= 4.5
Returns the average (arithmetic mean) of its arguments, which can be numbers or names, arrays, or references that contain numbers.
Number1: number1,number2,... are 1 to 255 numeric arguments for which you want the average.
Formula result = 4.5
Help on this function
OK Cancel

Here's what's in that dialog box:

- There's the name of the function, AVERAGE.
- Then there are text boxes where you enter the range of cells (the argument) on which you want the function to perform its duty (B1:B10). Notice that the actual numbers (2, 2, 5, 7, 5, 6, 3, 6, 5, 4) you want to average are listed to the right of the text box.
- Right below the argument boxes is the value the function will return to the cell in which it is located (which in this case is 4.5).
- In the middle of the dialog box (on the left) is what the function does (Returns the average . . .).
- Next is the syntax (or directions) of how to put the function together.
- The formula result (4.5) follows.
- Finally, there is a place to get help if you need it (Help on this function).

5. If Excel recognizes the data to which you want to apply the function, click OK and you are done. Otherwise, click on the RefEdit button and the Function Arguments box shrinks.

6. Drag the mouse over the range of cells (the data) you want included in the analysis. Click the RefEdit button.

7. Click the RefEdit button once again and then click OK. As you can see, the results are shown in the Function Arguments box and returned to the worksheet as you see in Figure A1. Also note that the syntax for the function appears in the formula bar.

More About the RefEdit Button and Collapsing and Expanding

Microsoft (the developer of Excel) thought it best to refer to the collapse and expand button as the RefEdit button. When the function dialog box is collapsed, clicking on the RefEdit button will expand the dialog box. When it is expanded, clicking on the RefEdit button will collapse it. It is as simple as that.

In sum, you use the RefEdit button to collapse and expand the function argument dialog box, and you are then able to drag the mouse over the cells that contain the information that the function arguments dialog box requires to complete the function.

Excel QuickGuide 1

The AVERAGE Function

What the AVERAGE Function Does

The AVERAGE function takes a set of values and computes the arithmetic mean, which is the sum of the values divided by the frequency of those values. It is the most often used measure of central tendency.

The Data Set

The data set used in this example is titled AVERAGE, and the question is, "What is the average speed of response and accuracy?"

Variable	*Description*
Response Time	Speed of response across 10 items
Accuracy	Number of items correct

Using the Average Function

1. **Click on the cell** where you want the AVERAGE function to be placed. (In the data set, the cell is C13.)
2. **Click Formulas → Insert Function** and you will see the Insert Function dialog box.
3. Locate and **double-click on the AVERAGE function** and you will see the Function Arguments dialog box as shown in Figure 1.1.
4. **Click the RefEdit button** in the Number1 entry box.
5. **Drag the mouse** over the range of cells (C2 through C11) you want included in the analysis.
6. **Click the RefEdit button** and press the return key or **click OK**. The AVERAGE function returns its value in Cell C13, as you see in Figure 1.2. Copy the function to Cell D13. The average response time is 6.92, and the average accuracy is 7.6. Note that you can see the syntax for the function in the formula bar at the top of the worksheet.

Related Functions: MODE, MEDIAN, GEOMEAN

Figure 1.1 The AVERAGE Function Arguments Dialog Box

Function Arguments

AVERAGE

Number1 =

Number2 = number

=

Returns the average (arithmetic mean) of its arguments, which can be numbers or names, arrays, or references that contain numbers.

Number1: number1,number2,... are 1 to 255 numeric arguments for which you want the average.

Formula result =

Help on this function

OK Cancel

Figure 1.2 The AVERAGE Function Returning the Mean Value

D13 *fx* =AVERAGE(D2:D11)

	A	B	C	D	E
1		ID	Response Time	Accuracy	
2		1	5.6	12	
3		2	7.3	3	
4		3	4.1	12	
5		4	6.8	7	
6		5	9.4	5	
7		6	10.4	2	
8		7	5.8	11	
9		8	7.8	7	
10		9	8.9	9	
11		10	3.1	8	
12					
13		AVERAGE	6.92	7.6	
14					

Excel QuickGuide 2

The MEDIAN Function

What the MEDIAN Function Does

The MEDIAN function computes the point at which 50% of the values fall above and 50% of the values fall below. It is most often used as a measure of central tendency when there are extreme scores.

The Data Set

The data set used in this example is titled MEDIAN, and the question is, "What is the median annual income for a group of 11 homeowners?"

Variable	*Description*
Income	Annual income in dollars

Using the MEDIAN Function

1. **Click on the cell** where you want the MEDIAN function to be placed. (In the data set, the cell is C14.)
2. **Click Formulas → Insert Function** and you will see the Insert Function dialog box.
3. Locate and **double-click on the MEDIAN function** and you will see the MEDIAN Function Arguments dialog box as shown in Figure 2.1.
4. **Click the RefEdit button** in the Number1 entry box.
5. **Drag the mouse** over the range of cells (C2 through C12) you want included in the analysis.
6. **Click the RefEdit button** and press the return key or **click OK**. The MEDIAN function returns its value in Cell C14, as you see in Figure 2.2. The median income value is $56,525. Note that you can see the syntax for the function in the formula bar at the top of the worksheet.

Related Functions: AVERAGE, MODE, GEOMEAN

Figure 2.1 The MEDIAN Function Arguments Dialog Box

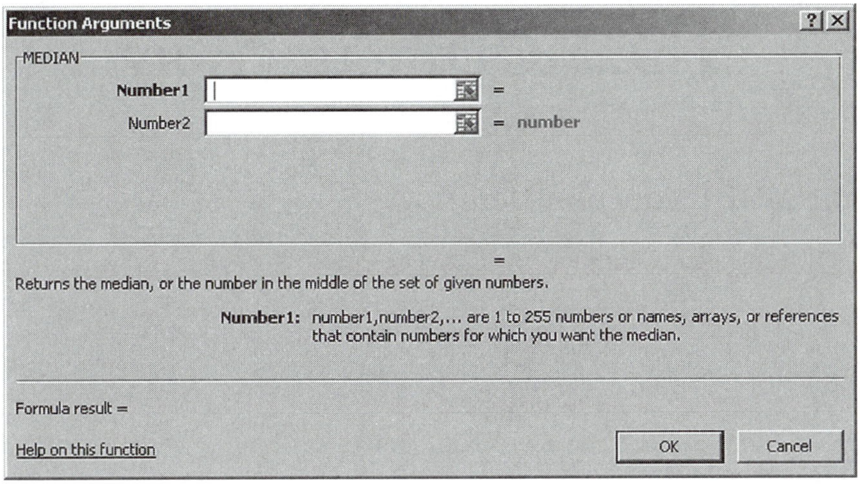

Function Arguments

MEDIAN

Number1 =

Number2 = number

=

Returns the median, or the number in the middle of the set of given numbers.

Number1: number1,number2,... are 1 to 255 numbers or names, arrays, or references that contain numbers for which you want the median.

Formula result =

Help on this function

OK Cancel

Figure 2.2 The MEDIAN Function Returning the Median Value

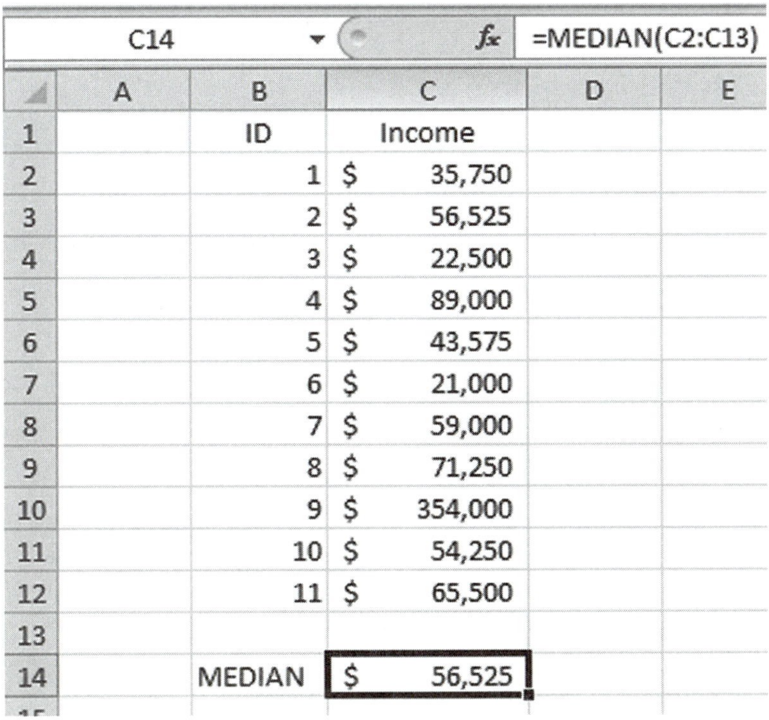

C14 *fx* =MEDIAN(C2:C13)

	A	B	C	D	E
1		ID	Income		
2		1	$ 35,750		
3		2	$ 56,525		
4		3	$ 22,500		
5		4	$ 89,000		
6		5	$ 43,575		
7		6	$ 21,000		
8		7	$ 59,000		
9		8	$ 71,250		
10		9	$ 354,000		
11		10	$ 54,250		
12		11	$ 65,500		
13					
14		MEDIAN	$ 56,525		

Excel QuickGuide 3

The MODE Function

What the MODE Function Does

The MODE function computes the most frequently occurring value in a set of values.

The Data Set

The data set used in this example is titled MODE, and the question is, "What is the mode or favorite flavor of ice cream?"

Variable	*Description*
Preference	1 = vanilla ice cream, 2 = strawberry ice cream, 3 = chocolate ice cream

Using the MODE Function

1. **Click on the cell** where you want the MODE function to be placed. (In the data set, the cell is C23.)
2. **Click Formulas → Insert Function** and you will see the Insert Function dialog box.
3. Locate and **double-click on the MODE function** and you will see the MODE Function Arguments dialog box as shown in Figure 3.1.
4. **Click the RefEdit button** in the Number1 entry box.
5. **Drag the mouse** over the range of cells (C2 through C21) you want included in the analysis.
6. **Click the RefEdit button** and press the return key or **click OK**. The MODE function returns its value in Cell C23, as you see in Figure 3.2. The MODE is 3 or the preference is for chocolate ice cream. Note that you can see the syntax for the function in the formula bar at the top of the worksheet.

Related Functions: AVERAGE, MEDIAN, GEOMEAN

Figure 3.1 The MODE Function Arguments Dialog Box

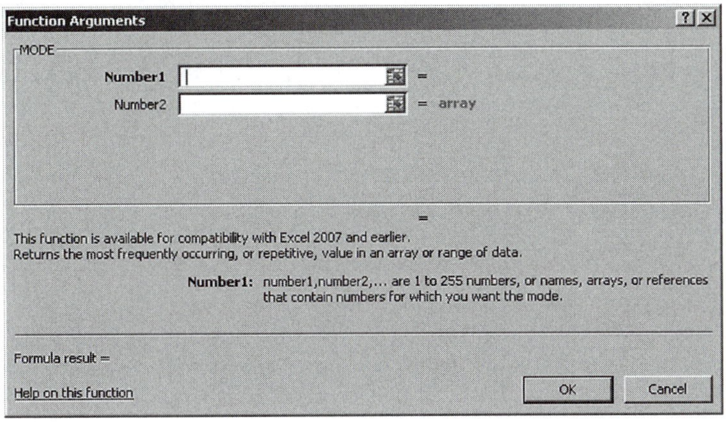

Function Arguments

MODE

Number1 =

Number2 = array

=

This function is available for compatibility with Excel 2007 and earlier.
Returns the most frequently occurring, or repetitive, value in an array or range of data.

Number1: number1,number2,... are 1 to 255 numbers, or names, arrays, or references that contain numbers for which you want the mode.

Formula result =

Help on this function

OK Cancel

Figure 3.2 The MODE Function Returning the Mode Value

C23 f_x =MODE(C2:C21)

	A	B	C	D	E
1		ID	Preference		
2		1	1		
3		2	2		
4		3	2		
5		4	2		
6		5	3		
7		6	3		
8		7	2		
9		8	2		
10		9	2		
11		10	3		
12		11	3		
13		12	3		
14		13	3		
15		14	3		
16		15	3		
17		16	3		
18		17	2		
19		18	3		
20		19	2		
21		20	1		
22					
23		MODE	3		

Excel QuickGuide 4

The GEOMEAN Function

What the GEOMEAN Function Does

The GEOMEAN function computes the geometric mean, used to compute an average of a set of numbers that are multiplied together.

The Data Set

The data set used in this example is titled GEOMEAN, and the question is, "What is the geometric mean for percent gains in achievement over a 5-year period?"

Variable	*Description*
Ach	Achievement gain for Years 1 through 5

Using the GEOMEAN Function

1. **Click on the cell** where you want the GEOMEAN function to be placed. (In the data set, the cell is C8.)
2. **Click Formulas → Insert Function** and you will see the Insert Function dialog box.
3. Locate and **double-click on the GEOMEAN function** and you will see the Function Arguments dialog box as shown in Figure 4.1.
4. **Click the RefEdit button** in the Number1 entry box.
5. **Drag the mouse** over the range of cells (C2 through C6) you want included in the analysis.
6. **Click the RefEdit button** and press the return key or **click OK**. The GEOMEAN function returns its value as .08 or 8% in Cell C8, as you see in Figure 4.2. Note that you can see the syntax for the function in the formula bar at the top of the worksheet.

Related Functions: AVERAGE, MEDIAN, MODE

Figure 4.1 The GEOMEAN Function Arguments Dialog Box

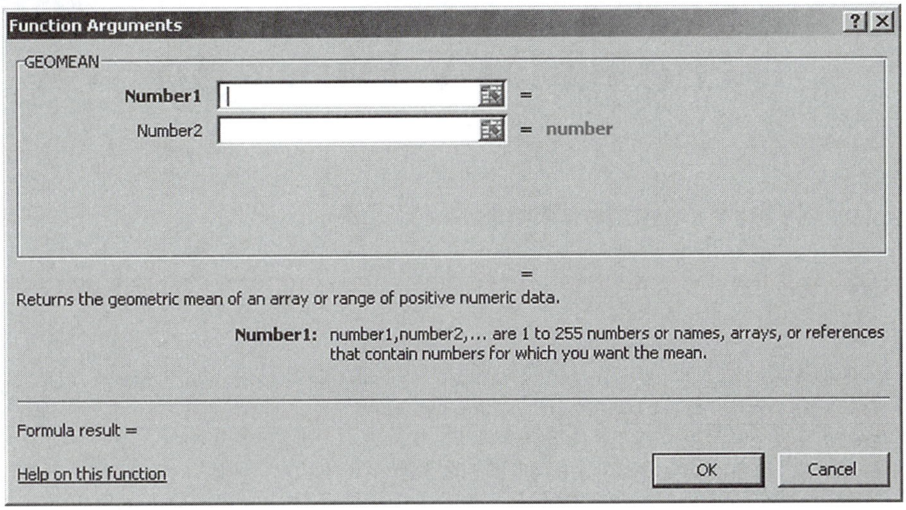

Function Arguments

GEOMEAN

Number1 =

Number2 = number

=

Returns the geometric mean of an array or range of positive numeric data.

Number1: number1,number2,... are 1 to 255 numbers or names, arrays, or references that contain numbers for which you want the mean.

Formula result =

Help on this function

OK Cancel

Figure 4.2 The GEOMEAN Function Returning the Geometric Mean

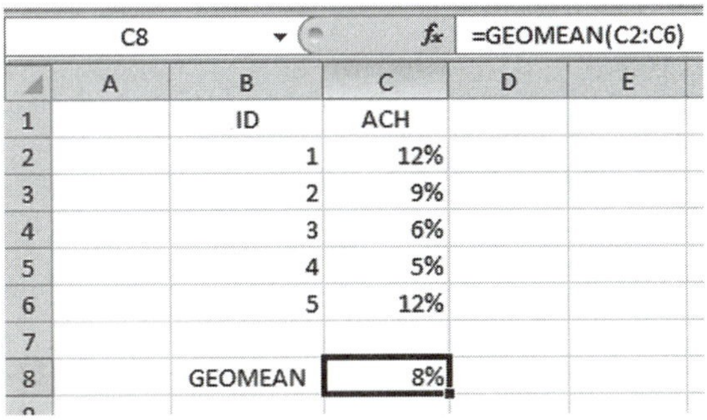

C8 f_x =GEOMEAN(C2:C6)

	A	B	C	D	E
1		ID	ACH		
2		1	12%		
3		2	9%		
4		3	6%		
5		4	5%		
6		5	12%		
7					
8		GEOMEAN	8%		

Excel QuickGuide 5

The STDEV Function

What the STDEV Function Does

The STDEV function takes a sample set of values and computes the standard deviation.

The Data Set

The data set used in this example is titled STDEV, and the question is, "What is the standard deviation for age for a sample of 20 sixth graders?"

Variable	*Description*
Age	Age in months

Using the STDEV Function

1. **Click on the cell** where you want the STDEV function to be placed. (In the data set, the cell is C23.)
2. **Click Formulas → Insert Function** and you will see the Insert Function dialog box.
3. Locate and **double-click on the STDEV function** and you will see the Function Arguments dialog box as shown in Figure 5.1.
4. **Click the RefEdit button** in the Number1 entry box.
5. **Drag the mouse** over the range of cells (C2 through C21) you want included in the analysis.
6. **Click the RefEdit button** and press the return key or **click OK**. The STDEV function returns its value as 4.99 in Cell C23, as you see in Figure 5.2. Note that you can see the syntax for the function in the formula bar at the top of the worksheet.

Related Functions: STDEVP, VAR, VARP

Figure 5.1 The STDEV Function Arguments Dialog Box

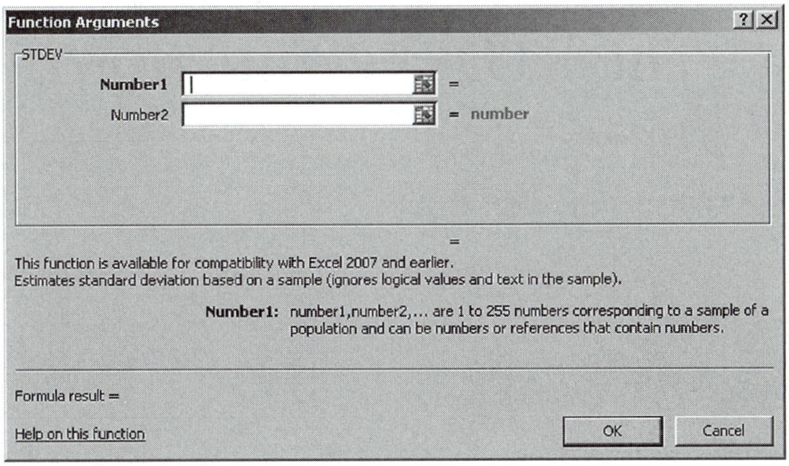

Function Arguments

STDEV

Number1 =

Number2 = number

=

This function is available for compatibility with Excel 2007 and earlier.
Estimates standard deviation based on a sample (ignores logical values and text in the sample).

Number1: number1,number2,... are 1 to 255 numbers corresponding to a sample of a population and can be numbers or references that contain numbers.

Formula result =

Help on this function

OK Cancel

Figure 5.2 The STDEV Function Returning the Standard Deviation for the Sample

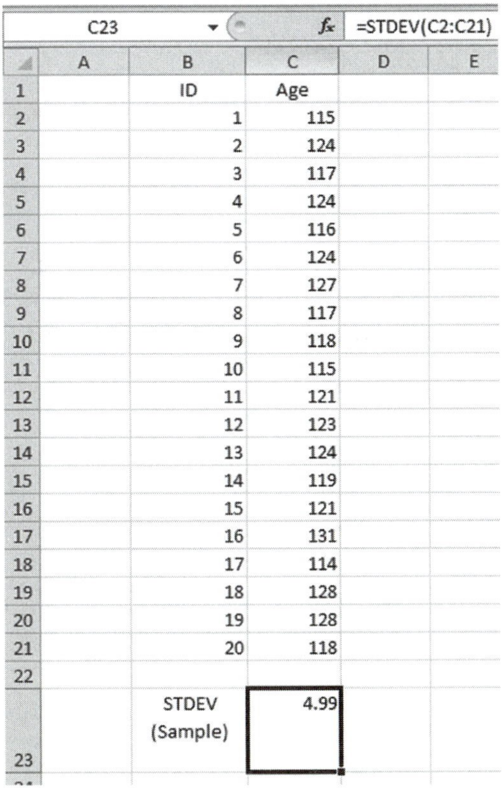

C23 *fx* =STDEV(C2:C21)

	A	B	C	D	E
1		ID	Age		
2		1	115		
3		2	124		
4		3	117		
5		4	124		
6		5	116		
7		6	124		
8		7	127		
9		8	117		
10		9	118		
11		10	115		
12		11	121		
13		12	123		
14		13	124		
15		14	119		
16		15	121		
17		16	131		
18		17	114		
19		18	128		
20		19	128		
21		20	118		
22					
23		STDEV (Sample)	4.99		

Excel QuickGuide 6

The STDEVP Function

What the STDEVP Function Does

The STDEVP function computes the standard deviation for scores from an entire population.

The Data Set

The data set used in this example is titled STDEVP, and the question is, "What is the standard deviation for the number of friendships lasting more than 1 year for a population of 90 10th graders?"

Variable	*Description*
Number of Friends	Number of friendships lasting more than 1 year for a group of adolescents.

Using the STDEVP Function

1. **Click on the cell** where you want the STDEVP function to be placed. (In the data set, the cell is C18.)
2. **Click Formulas → Insert Function** and you will see the Insert Function dialog box.
3. Locate and **double-click on the STDEVP function** and you will see the Function Arguments dialog box as shown in Figure 6.1.
4. **Click the RefEdit button** in the Number1 entry box.
5. **Drag the mouse** over the range of cells (C2 through H16) you want included in the analysis.
6. **Click the RefEdit button** and press the return key or **click OK**. The STDEVP function returns its value in Cell C18, as you see in Figure 6.2. The STDEVP for number of friends is 2.08. Note that you can see the syntax for the function in the formula bar at the top of the worksheet.

Related Functions: STDEV, VAR, VARP

Figure 6.1 The STDEVP Function Arguments Dialog Box

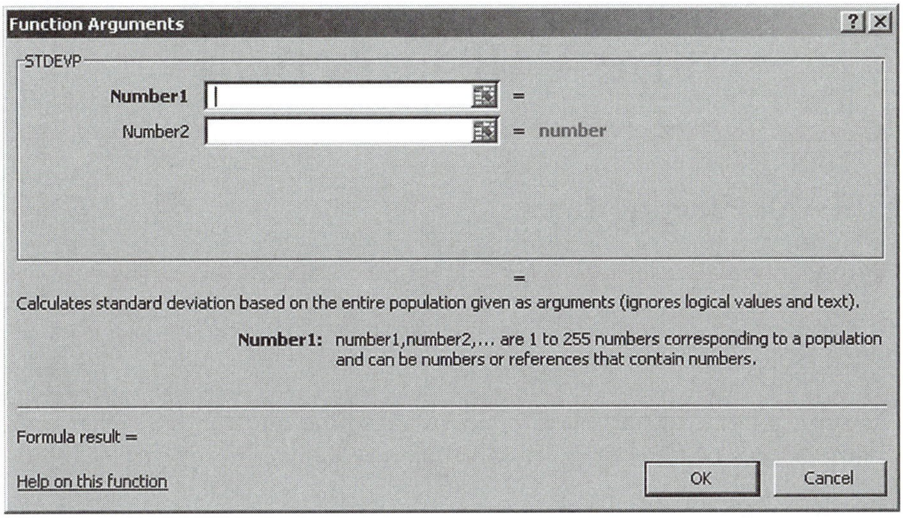

Function Arguments

STDEVP

Number1 =

Number2 = number

=

Calculates standard deviation based on the entire population given as arguments (ignores logical values and text).

Number1: number1,number2,... are 1 to 255 numbers corresponding to a population and can be numbers or references that contain numbers.

Formula result =

Help on this function

OK Cancel

Figure 6.2 The STDEVP Function Returning the Standard Deviation for the Population

C18 =STDEVP(C2:H16)

	A	B	C	D	E	F	G	H
1		ID	Number of Friends					
2		1	0	0	4	0	2	4
3		2	1	6	0	1	0	2
4		3	1	0	0	2	6	2
5		4	2	6	1	6	2	1
6		5	4	1	0	1	0	2
7		6	1	1	6	4	0	6
8		7	3	0	3	5	0	4
9		8	0	0	4	3	3	5
10		9	1	4	6	3	2	4
11		10	6	2	3	1	0	2
12		11	2	3	4	6	4	2
13		12	6	2	0	3	2	5
14		13	3	0	5	1	2	0
15		14	5	6	6	3	6	6
16		15	0	1	4	2	5	1
17								
18		STDEVP (Population)	2.08					

Excel QuickGuide 7

The VAR Function

What the VAR Function Does

The VAR function takes a sample set of values and computes the variance.

The Data Set

The data set used in this example is titled VAR, and the question is, "What is the variance for the scores on The Extroversion Scale (TES) for a sample of 20 high school seniors?"

Variable	*Description*
TES	Score on The Extroversion Scale ranging from 1 to 100

Using the VAR Function

1. **Click on the cell** where you want the VAR function to be placed. (In the data set, the cell is C23.)
2. **Click Formulas → Insert Function** and you will see the Insert Function dialog box.
3. Locate and **double-click on the VAR function** and you will see the Function Arguments dialog box as shown in Figure 7.1.
4. **Click the RefEdit button** in the Number1 entry box.
5. **Drag the mouse** over the range of cells (C2 through C21) you want included in the analysis.
6. **Click the RefEdit button** and press the return key or **click OK**. The VAR function returns its value as 246.37 in Cell C23, as you see in Figure 7.2. Note that you can see the syntax for the function in the formula bar at the top of the worksheet.

Related Functions: STDEV, STDEVP, VARP

Figure 7.1 The VAR Function Arguments Dialog Box

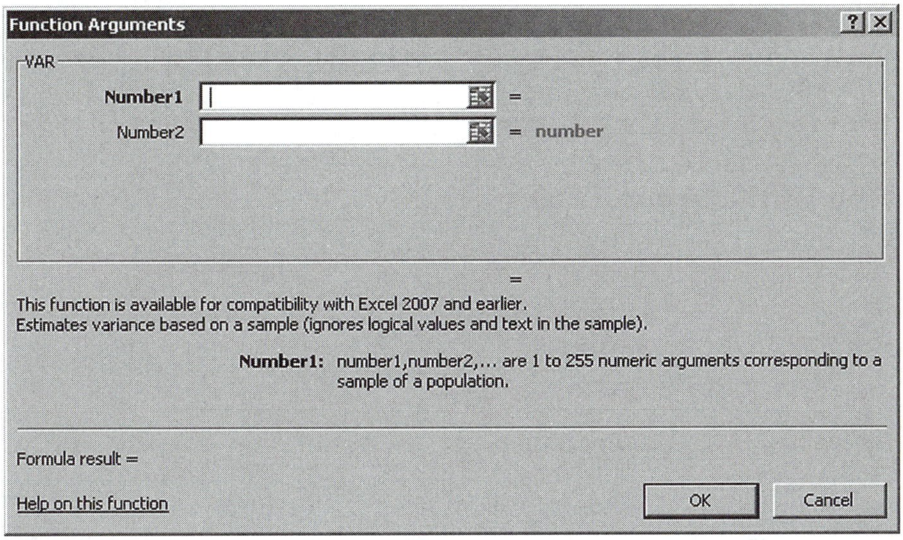

Function Arguments

VAR

Number1 =

Number2 = number

=

This function is available for compatibility with Excel 2007 and earlier.
Estimates variance based on a sample (ignores logical values and text in the sample).

Number1: number1,number2,... are 1 to 255 numeric arguments corresponding to a sample of a population.

Formula result =

Help on this function

OK Cancel

Figure 7.2 The VAR Function Returning the Variance for the Sample

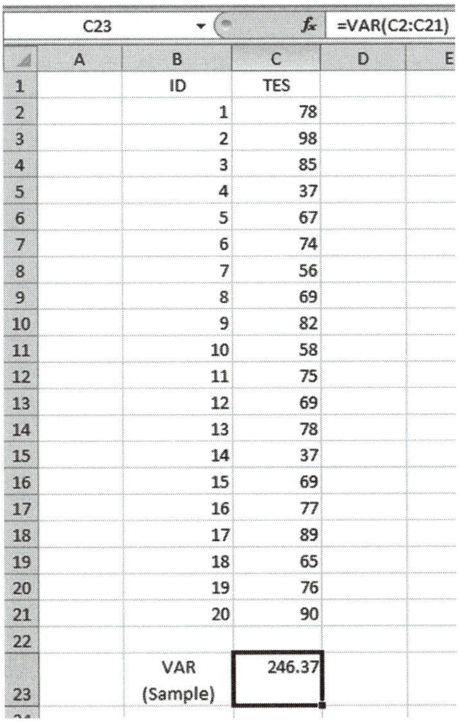

C23 fx =VAR(C2:C21)

	A	B	C	D	E
1		ID	TES		
2		1	78		
3		2	98		
4		3	85		
5		4	37		
6		5	67		
7		6	74		
8		7	56		
9		8	69		
10		9	82		
11		10	58		
12		11	75		
13		12	69		
14		13	78		
15		14	37		
16		15	69		
17		16	77		
18		17	89		
19		18	65		
20		19	76		
21		20	90		
22					
23		VAR (Sample)	246.37		

Excel QuickGuide 8

The VARP Function

What the VARP Function Does

The VARP function computes the variance for an entire population.

The Data Set

The data set used in this example is titled VARP, and the question is, "What is the variance for the scores on The Extroversion Scale (TES) for the population of 100 high school seniors?"

Variable	*Description*
TES	Score on The Extroversion Scale ranging from 1 to 100

Using the VARP Function

1. **Click on the cell** where you want the VARP function to be placed. (In the data set, the cell is C23.)
2. **Click Formulas → Insert Function** and you will see the Insert Function dialog box.
3. Locate and **double-click on the VARP function** and you will see the Function Arguments dialog box as shown in Figure 8.1.
4. **Click the RefEdit button** in the Number1 entry box.
5. **Drag the mouse** over the range of cells (C2 through G21) you want included in the analysis.
6. **Click the RefEdit button** and press the return key or **click OK**. The VARP function returns its value as 684.12 in Cell C23, as you see in Figure 8.2. Note that you can see the syntax for the function in the formula bar at the top of the worksheet.

Related Functions: STDEV, STDEVP, VAR

Figure 8.1 The VARP Function Arguments Dialog Box

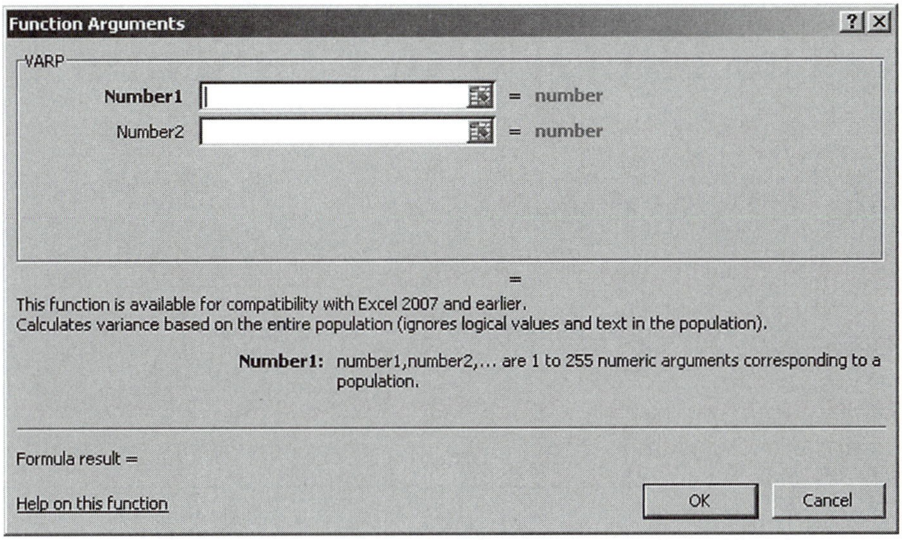

Function Arguments

VARP

Number1 = number

Number2 = number

=

This function is available for compatibility with Excel 2007 and earlier.
Calculates variance based on the entire population (ignores logical values and text in the population).

Number1: number1,number2,... are 1 to 255 numeric arguments corresponding to a population.

Formula result =

Help on this function

OK Cancel

Figure 8.2 The VARP Function Returning the Variance for the Population

C23 =VARP(C2:G21)

	A	B	C	D	E	F	G
1		ID	TES				
2		1	78	94	81	94	41
3		2	98	37	69	71	99
4		3	85	62	49	19	71
5		4	37	55	14	39	85
6		5	67	97	100	68	19
7		6	74	26	63	22	3
8		7	56	46	55	57	69
9		8	69	75	88	77	84
10		9	82	29	92	99	90
11		10	58	6	57	18	62
12		11	75	74	32	23	93
13		12	69	65	83	29	97
14		13	78	5	35	86	39
15		14	37	49	24	64	99
16		15	69	84	33	71	68
17		16	77	62	7	95	47
18		17	89	71	58	39	59
19		18	65	95	54	11	57
20		19	76	18	97	47	58
21		20	90	42	52	49	29
22							
23		VARP (Population)	684.12				

Excel QuickGuide 9

The FREQUENCY Function

What the FREQUENCY Function Does

The FREQUENCY function generates frequencies for a set of values.

The Data Set

The data set used in this example is titled FREQUENCY, and the question is, "What is the frequency of level of preference for TOOTS, a new type of cereal, by 50 consumers?"

Variable	*Description*
Preference	Preference on a scale from 1 through 5

Using the FREQUENCY Function

1. **Create the bins** (1, 2, 3, 4, and 5) into which you want the frequencies counted (as shown in Cells I2 through I6 in the Frequency data set).
2. **Highlight all the cells** (J2 through J6) where you want the frequencies to appear.
3. **Click Formulas → Insert Function** and you will see the Insert Function dialog box.
4. Locate and **double-click on the FREQUENCY function** and you will see the Function Arguments dialog box as shown in Figure 9.1.
5. **Click the RefEdit button** in the Data_array entry box and **drag the mouse** over the range of cells you want included in the analysis (B2 through G11). **Click the RefEdit button.**
6. **Click the RefEdit button** in the Bins_array entry box and drag the mouse over the range of cells that defines the bins (I2 through I6). **Click the RefEdit button.**
7. **Press the Ctrl + Shift + Return keys** in combination (not in a sequence). This is done because Excel treats Cells J2 through J6 as an array, not as a single value. In Figure 9.2, you can see the result of the function with frequencies listed beside the values in the bin. Note in the formula bar that the function is bounded by brackets {}, indicating the values are part of an array.

Related Functions: NORMDIST, PERCENTILE, PERCENTRANK, QUARTILE, RANK, STANDARDIZE

Figure 9.1 The FREQUENCY Function Arguments Dialog Box

Function Arguments

FREQUENCY

Data_array = reference

Bins_array = reference

=

Calculates how often values occur within a range of values and then returns a vertical array of numbers having one more element than Bins_array.

Data_array is an array of or reference to a set of values for which you want to count frequencies (blanks and text are ignored).

Formula result =

Help on this function

OK Cancel

Figure 9.2 The FREQUENCY Function Returning the Frequencies of Values

J2 *fx* {=FREQUENCY(B2:G11,I2:I6)}

	A	B	C	D	E	F	G	H	I	J
1		Preference							Bins	FREQUENCY
2		2	1	1	1	3	5		1	10
3		2	2	4	5	4	1		2	14
4		2	3	5	2	1	3		3	11
5		5	2	3	1	4	2		4	8
6		3	2	5	5	5	3		5	17
7		4	4	1	1	5	5			
8		1	4	2	3	2	3			
9		5	3	4	4	2	2			
10		5	2	5	5	5	1			
11		2	5	5	3	5	3			

Excel QuickGuide 10

The NORMDIST Function

What the NORMDIST Function Does

The NORMDIST function computes the cumulative probability of a score.

The Data Set

The data set used in this example is titled NORMDIST, and the question is, "What is the cumulative probability associated with a spelling test score of 9?"

Variable	*Description*
Spelling Score	Number of words spelled correctly out of 20

Using the NORMDIST Function

To use the NORMDIST function, follow these steps:

1. **Click on the cell** where you want the NORMDIST function to be placed. (In the data set, the cell is E2.)
2. **Click Formulas → Insert Function** and you will see the Insert Function dialog box.
3. Locate and **double-click on the NORMDIST function** and you will see the Function Arguments dialog box as shown in Figure 10.1.
4. For X, **click the RefEdit button** and enter the location of the value for which you want to compute the probability (in the data set, it is B2).
5. For the Mean and Standard_dev, **click the RefEdit button** and enter the appropriate cell addresses (B14 for the Mean and B15 for the Standard_dev).
6. For Cumulative, **type True**.
7. **Click OK** and the cumulative probability will be computed in Cell C2. In this example, the cumulative probability associated with a spelling score of 9 is .01 or 1%.
8. **Copy this result** from Cell D3 through Cell D12, and the results of the probabilities associated with scores from 9 through 19 will appear as shown in Figure 10.2.

Related Functions: FREQUENCY, PERCENTILE, PERCENTRANK, QUARTILE, RANK, STANDARDIZE

Figure 10.1 The NORMDIST Function Arguments Dialog Box

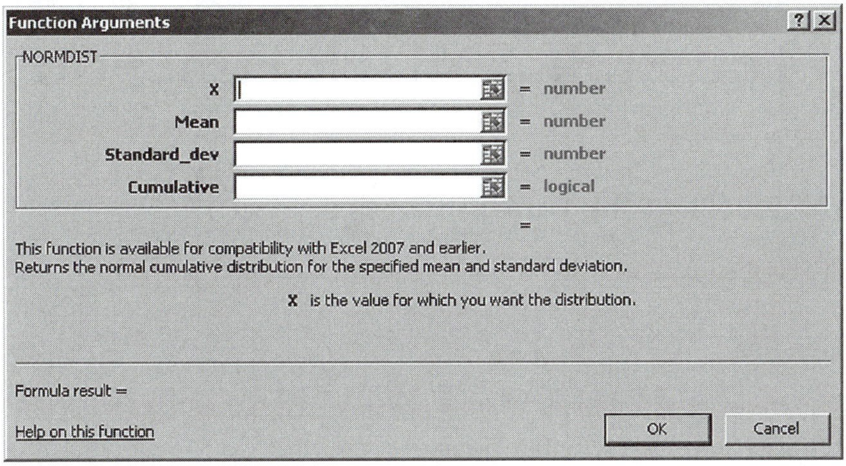

Function Arguments

NORMDIST

X = number

Mean = number

Standard_dev = number

Cumulative = logical

=

This function is available for compatibility with Excel 2007 and earlier.
Returns the normal cumulative distribution for the specified mean and standard deviation.

X is the value for which you want the distribution.

Formula result =

Help on this function

OK Cancel

Figure 10.2 The NORMDIST Function Returning the Cumulative Probability for a Set of Spelling Scores

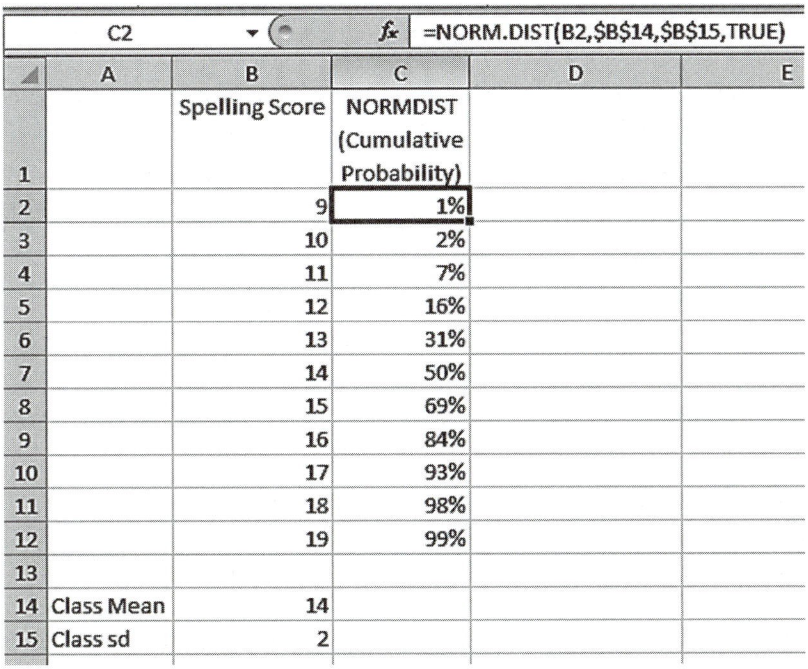

C2 *fx* =NORM.DIST(B2,B14,B15,TRUE)

	A	B	C	D	E
1		Spelling Score	NORMDIST (Cumulative Probability)		
2		9	1%		
3		10	2%		
4		11	7%		
5		12	16%		
6		13	31%		
7		14	50%		
8		15	69%		
9		16	84%		
10		17	93%		
11		18	98%		
12		19	99%		
13					
14	Class Mean	14			
15	Class sd	2			

Excel QuickGuide 11

The PERCENTILE Function

What the PERCENTILE Function Does

The PERCENTILE function computes the value for a defined percentile.

The Data Set

The data set used in this example is titled PERCENTILE, and the question is, "What are the percentile values for strength in a sample of twenty-five 55-year-olds?

Variable	*Description*
Strength	Amount of weight lifted

Using the PERCENTILE Function

1. **Click on the cell** where you want the PERCENTILE function to be placed. (In the data set, the cell is E2.)
2. **Click Formulas → Insert Function** and you will see the Insert Function dialog box.
3. Locate and **double-click on the PERCENTILE function** and you will see the Function Arguments dialog box as shown in Figure 11.1.
4. **Click the RefEdit button** in the Array entry box and **drag the mouse** over the range of cells (C2 through C26) you want included in the analysis. **Click the RefEdit button.**
5. **Click the RefEdit button** in the K entry box and **click on the cell (D2)** for which you want to compute the percentile value.
6. **Click the RefEdit button** and press the return key or **click OK**. The PERCENTILE function returns its value as 171 in Cell E2, as you see in Figure 11.2. The percentile values were then copied (using absolute references from Cell E2) from Cell E2 through Cell E11, as you see in Figure 11.2. Note that you can see the syntax for the function in the formula bar at the top of the worksheet.

Related Functions: FREQUENCY, NORMDIST, PERCENTRANK, QUARTILE, RANK, STANDARDIZE

Figure 11.1 The PERCENTILE Function Arguments Dialog Box

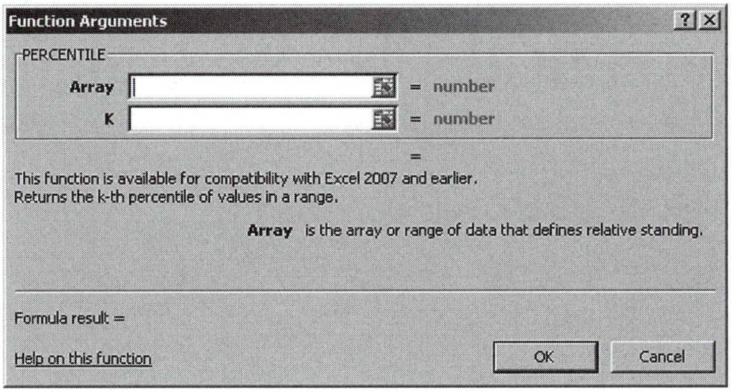

Function Arguments

PERCENTILE

Array = number

K = number

=

This function is available for compatibility with Excel 2007 and earlier.
Returns the k-th percentile of values in a range.

Array is the array or range of data that defines relative standing.

Formula result =

Help on this function

OK Cancel

Figure 11.2 The PERCENTILE Function Returning the Standard Deviation

E2 =PERCENTILE(C2:C26,D2)

	A	B	C	D	E	F
1		ID	Strength	Percentile	PERCENTILE (Value)	
2		1	149	100%	171.0	
3		2	142	90%	157.7	
4		3	117	80%	150.4	
5		4	132	70%	147.0	
6		5	152	60%	146.0	
7		6	171	50%	132.5	
8		7	134	40%	123.2	
9		8	166	30%	120.2	
10		9	101	20%	116.8	
11		10	147	10%	110.5	
12		11	148			
13		12	116			
14		13	105			
15		14	147			
16		15	157			
17		16	120			
18		17	122			
19		18	120			
20		19	146			
21		20	158			
22		21	100			
23		22	123			
24		23	131			
25		24	124			
26		25	145			
27						

Excel QuickGuide 12

The PERCENTRANK Function

What the PERCENTRANK Function Does

The PERCENTRANK function computes the percentage rank of a particular value in a data set.

The Data Set

The data set used in this example is titled PERCENTRANK, and the question is, "What is the percentile rank (or percentile) for the individual who lifts 149 pounds?"

Variable	*Description*
Strength	Amount of weight lifted

Using the PERCENTRANK Function

1. **Click on the cell** where you want the PERCENTRANK function to be placed. (In the data set, the cell is D2.)
2. **Click Formulas → Insert Function** and you will see the Insert Function dialog box.
3. Locate and **double-click on the PERCENTRANK function** and you will see the Function Arguments dialog box as shown in Figure 12.1.
4. **Click the RefEdit button** in the Array entry box.
5. **Drag the mouse** over the range of cells (C2 through C26) you want included in the analysis.
6. **Click the RefEdit button** in the X entry box.
7. **Click the X value** (Cell C2) for which you want to compute the PERCENTRANK or percentile rank.
8. **Click the RefEdit button** and press the return key or **click OK**. The PERCENTRANK function returns its value as 79% in Cell D2, as you see in Figure 12.2. The percentile values were then copied (using absolute references from Cell D2) from Cell D2 through Cell D26, as you see in Figure 12.2. Note that you can see the syntax for the function in the formula bar at the top of the worksheet.

Related Functions: FREQUENCY, NORMDIST, PERCENTILE, QUARTILE, RANK, STANDARDIZE

Figure 12.1 The PERCENTRANK Function Arguments Dialog Box

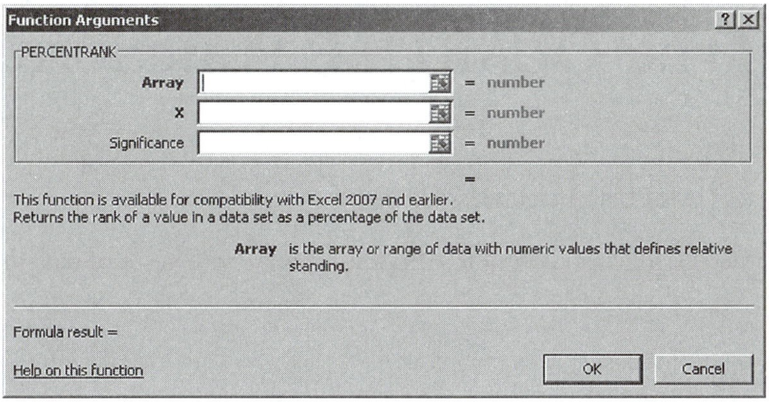

Function Arguments

PERCENTRANK

Array = number

X = number

Significance = number

=

This function is available for compatibility with Excel 2007 and earlier.
Returns the rank of a value in a data set as a percentage of the data set.

Array is the array or range of data with numeric values that defines relative standing.

Formula result =

Help on this function

OK Cancel

Figure 12.2 The PERCENTRANK Function Returning the Percentile Rank for the Set of Scores

D2 =PERCENTRANK(C2:C26,C2)

	A	B	C	D
1		ID	Strength	PERCENTRANK (Value)
2		1	149	79%
3		2	142	57%
4		3	117	18%
5		4	132	48%
6		5	152	80%
7		6	171	100%
8		7	134	56%
9		8	166	100%
10		9	101	6%
11		10	147	73%
12		11	148	86%
13		12	116	15%
14		13	105	8%
15		14	147	82%
16		15	157	90%
17		16	120	11%
18		17	122	25%
19		18	120	14%
20		19	146	83%
21		20	158	100%
22		21	100	0%
23		22	123	0%
24		23	131	50%
25		24	124	0%
26		25	145	100%
27				

Excel QuickGuide 13

The QUARTILE Function

What the QUARTILE Function Does

The QUARTILE function computes the values that divide a set of data into quartiles or fourths.

The Data Set

The data set used in this example is titled QUARTILE, and the question is, "What is the first quartile (or 25th percentile) in a set of health scores for a group of 25 nonsmokers?"

Variable	*Description*
Health Score	Risk of chronic illness score from 1 to 50

Using the QUARTILE Function

1. **Click on the cell** where you want the QUARTILE function to be placed. (In the data set, the cell is E2.)
2. **Click Formulas → Insert Function** and you will see the Insert Function dialog box.
3. Locate and **double-click on the QUARTILE function** and you will see the Function Arguments dialog box as shown in Figure 13.1.
4. **Click the RefEdit button** in the Array entry box.
5. **Drag the mouse** over the range of cells (C2 through C26) you want included in the analysis.
6. **Click the RefEdit button** in the X entry box.
7. **Click the Quart value** (Cell D2) to compute the 1st quartile.
8. **Click the RefEdit button** and press the return key or **click OK**. The QUARTILE function returns its value as 27 in Cell E2, as you see in Figure 13.2. The 2nd, 3rd, and 4th quartiles were computed as well. Note that you can see the syntax for the function in the formula bar at the top of the worksheet.

Related Functions: FREQUENCY, NORMDIST, PERCENTILE, PERCENTRANK, RANK, STANDARDIZE

Figure 13.1 The QUARTILE Function Arguments Dialog Box

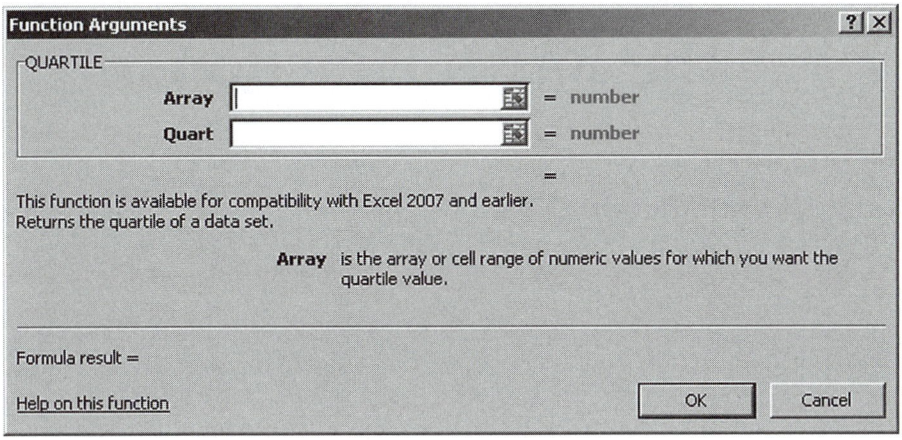

Function Arguments

QUARTILE

Array = number

Quart = number

=

This function is available for compatibility with Excel 2007 and earlier.
Returns the quartile of a data set.

Array is the array or cell range of numeric values for which you want the quartile value.

Formula result =

Help on this function

OK Cancel

Figure 13.2 The QUARTILE Function Returning the Quartile for a Set of Scores

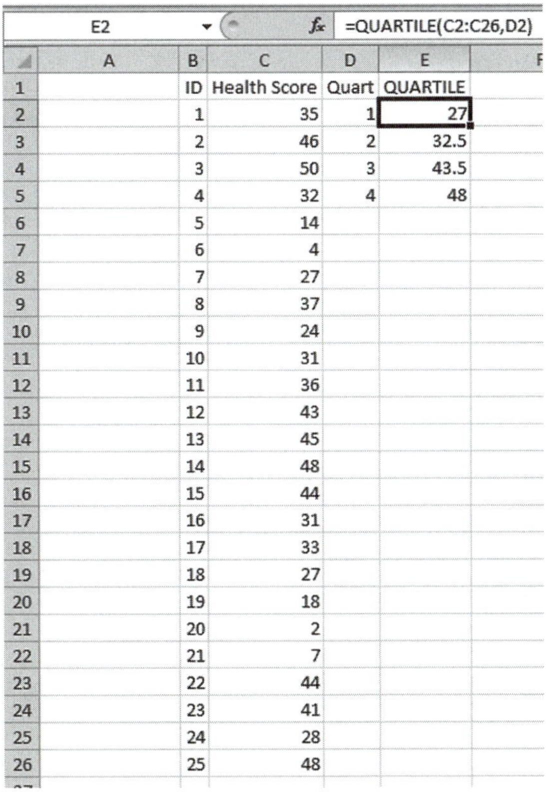

E2 =QUARTILE(C2:C26,D2)

	A	B	C	D	E
1		ID	Health Score	Quart	QUARTILE
2		1	35	1	27
3		2	46	2	32.5
4		3	50	3	43.5
5		4	32	4	48
6		5	14		
7		6	4		
8		7	27		
9		8	37		
10		9	24		
11		10	31		
12		11	36		
13		12	43		
14		13	45		
15		14	48		
16		15	44		
17		16	31		
18		17	33		
19		18	27		
20		19	18		
21		20	2		
22		21	7		
23		22	44		
24		23	41		
25		24	28		
26		25	48		

Excel QuickGuide 14

The RANK Function

What the RANK Function Does

The RANK function computes the percentage rank of a particular value in a data set.

The Data Set

The data set used in this example is titled RANK, and the question is, "What is the relative rank for a set of 20 grade point averages?"

Variable	*Description*
GPA	Grade point average

Using the RANK Function

1. **Click on the cell** where you want the RANK function to be placed. (In the data set, the cell is D2.)
2. **Click Formulas → Insert Function** and you will see the Insert Function dialog box.
3. Locate and **double-click the RANK function** and you will see the Function Arguments dialog box as shown in Figure 14.1.
4. **Click the RefEdit button** in the Number entry box and **click the value** for which you want to compute the rank (Cell C2).
5. **Click the RefEdit button** in the Ref entry box and **drag the mouse** over the array of values being ranked (C2 through C21).
6. **Click the RefEdit button** and press the return key or **click OK**. The RANK function returns its value as 5 in Cell D2 (for a GPA of 3.4), as you see in Figure 14.2. The ranks for all the other data points were computed as well. Note that you can see the syntax for the function in the formula bar at the top of the worksheet.

Related Functions: FREQUENCY, NORMDIST, PERCENTILE, PERCENTRANK, QUARTILE, STANDARDIZE

Figure 14.1 The RANK Function Arguments Dialog Box

Function Arguments

RANK

Number = number

Ref = reference

Order = logical

=

This function is available for compatibility with Excel 2007 and earlier.
Returns the rank of a number in a list of numbers: its size relative to other values in the list.

Number is the number for which you want to find the rank.

Formula result =

Help on this function

OK Cancel

Figure 14.2 The RANK Function Returning the Rank for a Set of Scores

D2 =RANK(C2:C21,C2:C21)

	A	B	C	D
1		ID	GPA	RANK
2		1	3.4	5
3		2	3.9	1
4		3	2.4	10
5		4	2.1	12
6		5	2.8	7
7		6	1.7	13
8		7	2.3	10
9		8	3.3	4
10		9	3.5	2
11		10	1.6	10
12		11	3.8	1
13		12	3.1	2
14		13	2.6	3
15		14	3.5	1
16		15	1.5	6
17		16	2.1	4
18		17	2.5	2
19		18	2.4	2
20		19	3.1	1
21		20	2.0	1

Excel QuickGuide 15

The STANDARDIZE Function

What the STANDARDIZE Function Does

The STANDARDIZE function computes a normalized or standard score.

The Data Set

The data set used in this example is titled STANDARDIZE, and the question is, "What are the normalized scores for a set of raw test scores on the INT, a measure of introversion?"

Variable	*Description*
INT	A measure of introversion ranging from 1 to 25

Using the STANDARDIZE Function

1. **Click on the cell** where you want the STANDARDIZE function to be placed. (In the data set, the cell is D2.)
2. **Click Formulas → Insert Function** and you will see the Insert Function dialog box.
3. Locate and **double-click the STANDARDIZE function** and you will see the Function Arguments dialog box as shown in Figure 15.1.
4. **Click the RefEdit button** in the X entry box and **click the value** for which you want to compute STANDARDIZE (Cell C2). **Click the RefEdit button.**
5. **Click the RefEdit button** in the Mean entry box and click the mean of the values being standardized (Cell C23). **Click the RefEdit button.**
6. **Click the RefEdit button** in the Standard_dev entry box and click the STDEV of the values being standardized (Cell C24). **Click the RefEdit button.**
7. **Click the RefEdit button** and press the return key or **click OK**. The STANDARDIZE function returns its value as –0.58 in Cell D2, as you see in Figure 15.2. The standardized scores for all the other data points were computed (each one individually and not copied down). The syntax for the function in the formula bar is shown at the top of the worksheet.

Related Functions: FREQUENCY, NORMDIST, PERCENTILE, PERCENTRANK, QUARTILE, RANK

Figure 15.1 The STANDARDIZE Function Arguments Dialog Box

Function Arguments

STANDARDIZE

X = number

Mean = number

Standard_dev = number

=

Returns a normalized value from a distribution characterized by a mean and standard deviation.

X is the value you want to normalize.

Formula result =

Help on this function

OK Cancel

Figure 15.2 The STANDARDIZE Function Returning Standardized Values for a Set of Scores

D2 =STANDARDIZE(C2,C23,C24)

	A	B	C	D
1		ID	INT	STANDARDIZE
2		1	12	-0.58
3		2	15	-0.08
4		3	14	-0.24
5		4	21	0.93
6		5	23	1.26
7		6	25	1.59
8		7	7	-1.41
9		8	15	-0.08
10		9	21	0.93
11		10	8	-1.24
12		11	22	1.09
13		12	15	-0.08
14		13	14	-0.24
15		14	22	1.09
16		15	19	0.59
17		16	17	0.26
18		17	9	-1.08
19		18	10	-0.91
20		19	3	-2.08
21		20	17	0.26
22				
23		AVERAGE	15.45	
24		STDEV	6.00	
25				

Excel QuickGuide 16

The COVAR Function

What the COVAR Function Does

The COVAR function takes a set of paired values and estimates how much two variables change together.

The Data Set

The data set used in this example is titled COVAR, and the question is, "What is the relationship between level of intervention and number of injuries in college athletes?"

Variable	*Description*
Intervention	Hours of training
Injuries	Number of injuries

Using the COVAR Function

1. **Click on the cell** where you want the COVAR function to be placed. (In the data set, the cell is D23.)
2. **Click Formulas → Insert Function** and you will see the Insert Function dialog box.
3. Locate and **double-click on the COVAR function** and you will see the Function Arguments dialog box as shown in Figure 16.1.
4. **Click the RefEdit button** in the Array 1 entry box and **drag the mouse** over the range of cells (C2 through C21) you want included in the analysis. **Click the RefEdit button**.
5. **Repeat Steps 3 and 4** for Array 2 (Cells D2 through D21) and **click the RefEdit button** and press the return key or **click OK**. The COVAR function returns its value as –1.81 in Cell D23, as you see in Figure 16.2. You can see the syntax for the function in the formula bar at the top of the worksheet.

Related Functions: CORREL, PEARSON, INTERCEPT, SLOPE, TREND, FORECAST, RSQ

Figure 16.1 The COVAR Function Arguments Dialog Box

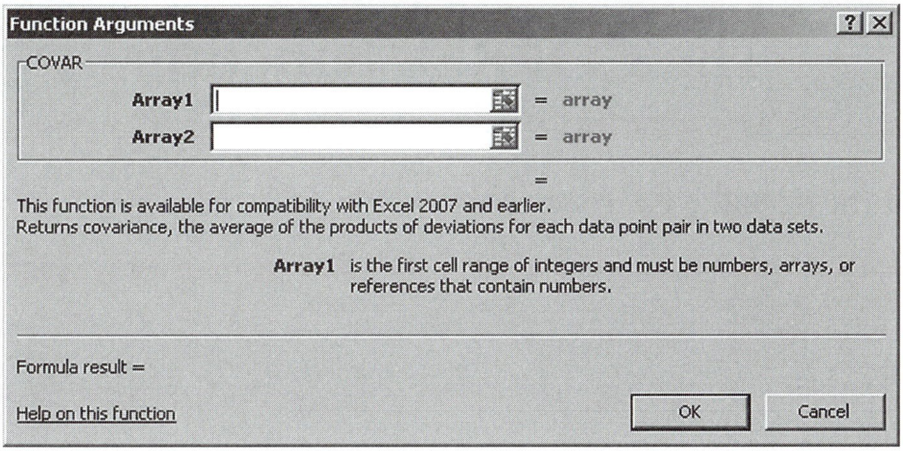

Function Arguments

COVAR

Array1 = array

Array2 = array

=

This function is available for compatibility with Excel 2007 and earlier.
Returns covariance, the average of the products of deviations for each data point pair in two data sets.

Array1 is the first cell range of integers and must be numbers, arrays, or references that contain numbers.

Formula result =

Help on this function

OK Cancel

Figure 16.2 The COVAR Function Returning the Function's Value

D23 =COVAR(C2:C21,D2:D21)

	A	B	C	D	E
1		ID	Intervention	Injuries	
2		1	6	4	
3		2	7	5	
4		3	5	6	
5		4	8	7	
6		5	7	6	
7		6	7	8	
8		7	6	6	
9		8	5	5	
10		9	6	4	
11		10	7	8	
12		11	8	7	
13		12	8	7	
14		13	9	1	
15		14	8	3	
16		15	7	2	
17		16	6	4	
18		17	4	8	
19		18	3	7	
20		19	2	9	
21		20	5	9	
22					
23		COVAR		-1.81	

Excel QuickGuide 17

The CORREL Function

What the CORREL Function Does

The CORREL function computes the value of the Pearson product-moment correlation between two variables.

The Data Set

The data set used in this example is titled CORREL, and the question is, "What is the correlation between height and weight for 20 sixth graders?"

Variable	*Description*
Height	Height in inches
Weight	Weight in pounds

Using the CORREL Function

1. **Click on the cell** where you want the CORREL function to be placed. (In the data set, the cell is C23.)
2. **Click Formulas → Insert Function** and you will see the Insert Function dialog box.
3. Locate and **double-click on the CORREL function** and you will see the Function Arguments dialog box as shown in Figure 17.1.
4. **Click the RefEdit button** in the Array 1 entry box and **drag the mouse** over the range of cells (C2 through C21) you want included in the analysis. **Click the RefEdit button.**
5. **Repeat Steps 3 and 4** for Array 2 (Cells D2 through D21) and then **click the RefEdit button** and **click OK**. The CORREL function returns its value as .78 in Cell C23, as you see in Figure 17.2. You can see the syntax for the function in the formula bar at the top of the worksheet.

Related Functions: COVAR, PEARSON, INTERCEPT, SLOPE, TREND, FORECAST, RSQ

Figure 17.1 The CORREL Function Arguments Dialog Box

Function Arguments

CORREL

Array1 = array

Array2 = array

=

Returns the correlation coefficient between two data sets.

Array1 is a cell range of values. The values should be numbers, names, arrays, or references that contain numbers.

Formula result =

Help on this function

OK Cancel

Figure 17.2 The CORREL Function Returning the Correlation

C23 =CORREL(C2:C21,D2:D21)

	A	B	C	D	E	F
1		ID	Height	Weight		
2		1	60	134		
3		2	63	143		
4		3	71	156		
5		4	58	121		
6		5	61	131		
7		6	59	117		
8		7	64	125		
9		8	67	126		
10		9	63	143		
11		10	52	98		
12		11	61	154		
13		12	58	125		
14		13	54	109		
15		14	61	117		
16		15	64	126		
17		16	63	154		
18		17	49	98		
19		18	59	143		
20		19	69	144		
21		20	71	156		
22						
23		CORREL	0.78			

Excel QuickGuide 18

The PEARSON Function

What the PEARSON Function Does

The PEARSON function computes the value of the Pearson product-moment correlation between two variables.

The Data Set

The data set used in this example is titled PEARSON, and the question is, "What is the correlation between income and level of education for 20 households?"

Variable	*Description*
Income	Annual income in dollars
Level of Education	Years of education

Using the PEARSON Function

1. **Click on the cell** where you want the PEARSON function to be placed. (In the data set, the cell is C23.)
2. **Click Formulas → Insert Function** and you will see the Insert Function dialog box.
3. Locate and **double-click on the PEARSON function** and you will see the Function Arguments dialog box as shown in Figure 18.1.
4. **Click the RefEdit button** in the Array 1 entry box and **drag the mouse** over the range of cells (C2 through C21) you want included in the analysis. **Click the RefEdit button.**
5. **Repeat Steps 3 and 4** for Array 2 (Cells D2 through D21) and then **click the RefEdit button** and **click OK**. The PEARSON function returns its value as .76 in Cell C23, as you see in Figure 18.2. You can see the syntax for the function in the formula bar at the top of the worksheet.

Related Functions: COVAR, CORREL, INTERCEPT, SLOPE, TREND, FORECAST, RSQ

Figure 18.1 The PEARSON Function Arguments Dialog Box

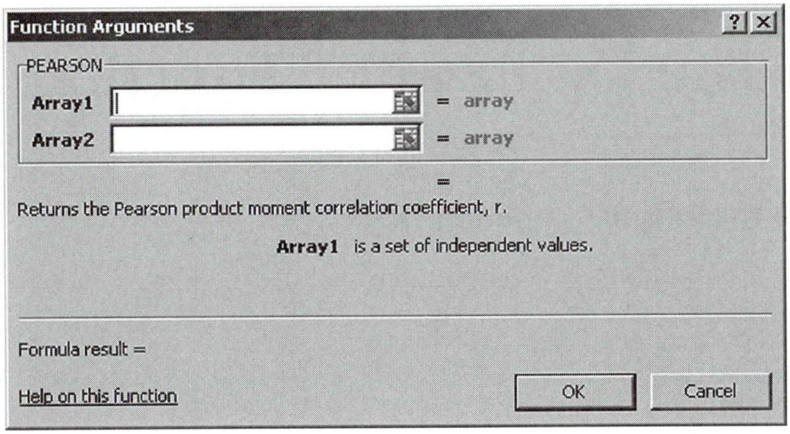

Function Arguments

PEARSON

Array1		= array
Array2		= array

=

Returns the Pearson product moment correlation coefficient, r.

Array1 is a set of independent values.

Formula result =

Help on this function

OK Cancel

Figure 18.2 The PEARSON Function Returning the Correlation

C23 f_x =PEARSON(C2:C21,D2:D21)

	A	B	C	D	E
1		ID	Income	Level of Education	
2		1	$ 59,602	9	
3		2	$ 57,108	9	
4		3	$ 42,027	6	
5		4	$ 58,404	7	
6		5	$ 50,731	6	
7		6	$ 34,054	8	
8		7	$ 51,579	9	
9		8	$ 30,445	3	
10		9	$ 35,052	2	
11		10	$ 35,976	4	
12		11	$ 57,250	10	
13		12	$ 37,526	4	
14		13	$ 39,274	2	
15		14	$ 55,613	9	
16		15	$ 46,775	7	
17		16	$ 30,552	5	
18		17	$ 51,331	9	
19		18	$ 54,391	8	
20		19	$ 36,178	1	
21		20	$ 41,616	2	
22					
23		PEARSON	0.76		

Excel QuickGuide 19

The INTERCEPT Function

What the INTERCEPT Function Does

The INTERCEPT function computes the intercept value, the point at which the regression line crosses the *y*-axis.

The Data Set

The data set used in this example is titled INTERCEPT, and the question is, "What is the intercept for the regression line for wins predicted by injuries for 15 teams?"

Variable	*Description*
Wins (*Y*)	Number of wins last season
Injuries (*X*)	Average number of weekly injuries

Using the INTERCEPT Function

1. **Click on the cell** where you want the INTERCEPT function to be placed. (In the data set, the cell is C18.)
2. **Click Formulas → Insert Function** and you will see the Insert Function dialog box.
3. Locate and **double-click on the INTERCEPT function** and you will see the Function Arguments dialog box as shown in Figure 19.1.
4. **Click the RefEdit button** in the Known_y's entry box and **drag the mouse** over the range of cells (D2 through D16) you want included in the analysis. **Click the RefEdit button.**
5. **Repeat Steps 3 and 4** for Known_x's (Cells C2 through C16) and then **click the RefEdit button** and **click OK**. The INTERCEPT function returns its value as 4.52 in Cell C18, as you see in Figure 19.2. You can see the syntax for the function in the formula bar at the top of the worksheet.

Related Functions: COVAR, CORREL, PEARSON, SLOPE, TREND, FORECAST, RSQ

Figure 19.1 The INTERCEPT Function Arguments Dialog Box

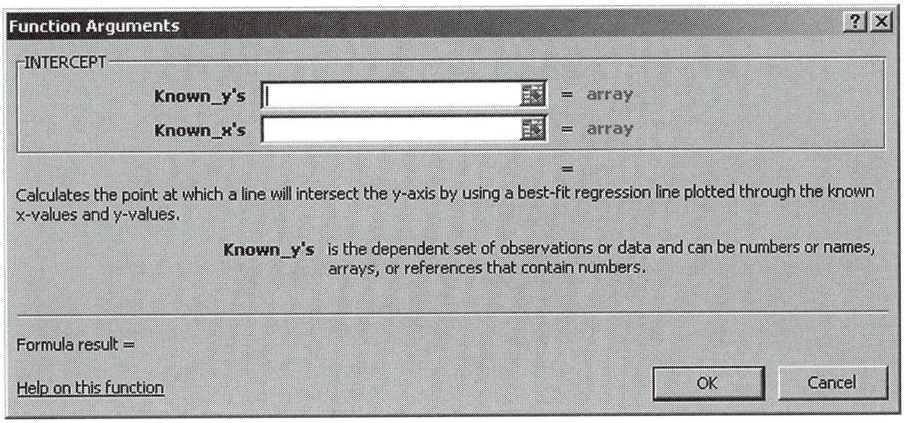

Function Arguments

INTERCEPT

Known_y's = array

Known_x's = array

=

Calculates the point at which a line will intersect the y-axis by using a best-fit regression line plotted through the known x-values and y-values.

Known_y's is the dependent set of observations or data and can be numbers or names, arrays, or references that contain numbers.

Formula result =

Help on this function

OK Cancel

Figure 19.2 The INTERCEPT Function Returning the Value of the Intercept

C18 =INTERCEPT(D2:D16,C2:C16)

	A	B	C	D	E	F
1		Team ID	Injuries (X)	Wins (Y)		
2		1	8	9		
3		2	7	9		
4		3	9	6		
5		4	8	7		
6		5	7	6		
7		6	4	8		
8		7	8	9		
9		8	11	3		
10		9	5	2		
11		10	2	4		
12		11	14	10		
13		12	7	4		
14		13	6	2		
15		14	4	9		
16		15	9	7		
17						
18		INTERCEPT	4.52			

Excel QuickGuide 20

The SLOPE Function

What the SLOPE Function Does

The SLOPE function computes the slope of the regression line.

The Data Set

The data set used in this example is titled SLOPE, and the question is, "What is the slope of the regression line that predicts wins from injuries?"

Variable	*Description*
Wins (*Y*)	Number of wins last season
Injuries (*X*)	Average number of weekly injuries

Using the SLOPE Function

1. **Highlight the cell** where you want the value of the SLOPE function to be returned. (In the data set, it is C18.)
2. **Click Formulas → Insert Function** and you will see the Insert Function dialog box.
3. Locate and **double-click on the SLOPE function** and you will see the Function Arguments dialog box as shown in Figure 20.1.
4. **Click the RefEdit button** in the Known_y's entry box and **drag the mouse** over the range of cells (D2 through D16) you want included in the analysis. **Click the RefEdit button.**
5. **Repeat Steps 3 and 4** for Known_x's (Cells C2 through C16) and then **click the RefEdit button** and **click OK**. The SLOPE function returns its value as .25 in Cell C18, as you see in Figure 20.2. You can see the syntax for the function in the formula bar at the top of the worksheet.

Related Functions: COVAR, CORREL, PEARSON, INTERCEPT, TREND, FORECAST, RSQ

Figure 20.1 The SLOPE Function Arguments Dialog Box

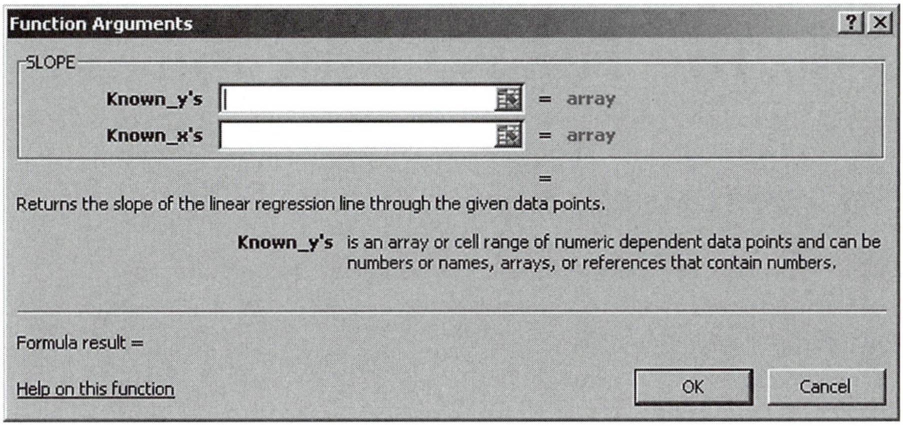

Function Arguments

SLOPE

Known_y's = array

Known_x's = array

=

Returns the slope of the linear regression line through the given data points.

Known_y's is an array or cell range of numeric dependent data points and can be numbers or names, arrays, or references that contain numbers.

Formula result =

Help on this function

OK Cancel

Figure 20.2 The SLOPE Function Returning the Slope of the Regression Line

C18 *fx* =SLOPE(D2:D16,C2:C16)

	A	B	C	D	E	F
1		Team ID	Injuries (X)	Wins (Y)		
2		1	8	9		
3		2	7	9		
4		3	9	6		
5		4	8	7		
6		5	7	6		
7		6	4	8		
8		7	8	9		
9		8	11	3		
10		9	5	2		
11		10	2	4		
12		11	14	10		
13		12	7	4		
14		13	6	2		
15		14	4	9		
16		15	9	7		
17						
18		SLOPE	0.25			

Excel QuickGuide 21

The TREND Function

What the TREND Function Does

The TREND function uses the regression line values to predict outcomes.

The Data Set

The data set used in this example is titled TREND, and the question is, "What is the predicted level of wins given injuries for members of 15 volleyball teams?"

Variable	*Description*
Injuries (*X*)	Average number of player injuries
Wins (*Y*)	Season wins

Using the TREND Function

1. **Highlight the cells** where you want the array of TREND values to appear. (In the data set, the cells are F2 through F4.)
2. **Click Formulas → Insert Function** and you will see the Insert Function dialog box.
3. Locate and **double-click on the TREND function** and you will see the Function Arguments dialog box as shown in Figure 21.1.
4. **Click the RefEdit button** in the Known_y's entry box and **drag the mouse** over the range of cells (D2 through D16) you want included in the analysis. **Click the RefEdit button.**
5. **Click the RefEdit button** for Known_x's (Cells C2 through C16) and then **click the RefEdit button**.
6. **Click the RefEdit button** for New_x's (Cells E2 through E4) and then **click the RefEdit button**.
7. Because this is an array, **use the Ctrl + Shift + Return key combination** to produce the TREND function and three predicted scores of 5.27, 4.77, and 7.02, as you see in Figure 21.2. You can see the syntax for the function in the formula bar at the top of the worksheet.

Related Functions: COVAR, CORREL, PEARSON, INTERCEPT, SLOPE, FORECAST, RSQ

Figure 21.1 The TREND Function Arguments Dialog Box

Function Arguments

TREND

Known_y's		= reference
Known_x's		= reference
New_x's		= reference
Const		= logical

=

Returns numbers in a linear trend matching known data points, using the least squares method.

Known_y's is a range or array of y-values you already know in the relationship y = mx + b.

Formula result =

Help on this function

OK Cancel

Figure 21.2 The TREND Function Returning the Trend of the Regression Line

F2 *fx* {=TREND(D2:D16,C2:C16,E2:E4)}

	A	B	C	D	E	F
1		Team ID	Injuries (X)	Wins (Y)	New Injuries	TREND
2		1	8	9	3	5.27
3		2	7	9	1	4.77
4		3	9	6	10	7.02
5		4	8	7		
6		5	7	6		
7		6	4	8		
8		7	8	9		
9		8	11	3		
10		9	5	2		
11		10	2	4		
12		11	14	10		
13		12	7	4		
14		13	6	2		
15		14	4	9		
16		15	9	7		

Excel QuickGuide 22

The FORECAST Function

What the FORECAST Function Does

The FORECAST function computes a predicted value for known values of *X*.

The Data Set

The data set used in this example is titled FORECAST, and the question is, "What is the predicted GPA for nine newly ranked high school students?"

Variable	*Description*
GPA (*Y*)	Grade point average
Rank (*X*)	High school rank (from 1 to 5)

Using the FORECAST Function

1. **Highlight the cells** where you want the array of FORECAST values to appear. (In the data set, the cells are F2 through F10.)
2. **Click Formulas → Insert Function** and you will see the Insert Function dialog box.
3. Locate and **double-click on the FORECAST function** and you will see the Function Arguments dialog box as shown in Figure 22.1.
4. **Click the RefEdit button** in the X entry box and **drag the mouse** over the range of cells (E2 through E10) you are using to predict the Y. **Click the RefEdit button.**
5. **Click the RefEdit button** in the Known_y's entry box and **drag the mouse** over the range of cells (C2 through C26) you want included in the analysis. **Click the RefEdit button.**
6. **Click the RefEdit button** in the Known_x's entry box and **drag the mouse** over the range of cells (D2 through D26) you want included in the analysis. **Click the RefEdit button.**
7. Because this is an array, **press the Ctrl + Shift + Return key combination** to produce the FORECAST function and the forecast scores of 3.51, 3.20, and so on, as you see in Figure 22.2. You can see the syntax for the function in the formula bar at the top of the worksheet.

Related Functions: COVAR, CORREL, PEARSON, INTERCEPT, SLOPE, TREND, RSQ

Figure 22.1 The FORECAST Function Arguments Dialog Box

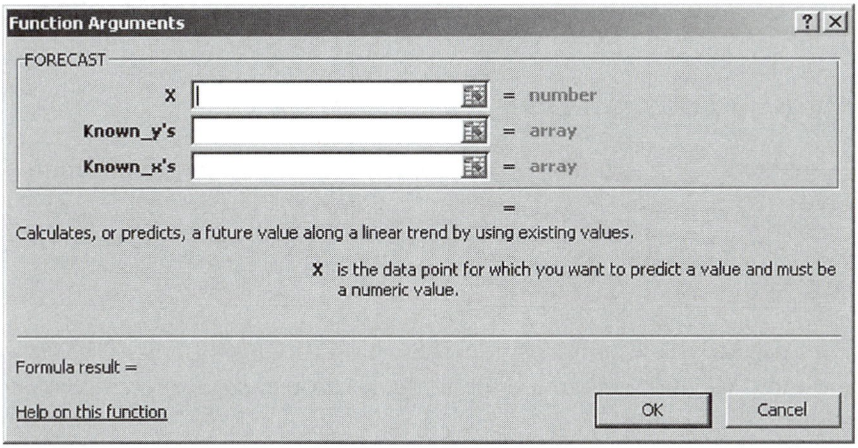

Function Arguments

FORECAST

X = number

Known_y's = array

Known_x's = array

=

Calculates, or predicts, a future value along a linear trend by using existing values.

X is the data point for which you want to predict a value and must be a numeric value.

Formula result =

Help on this function

OK Cancel

Figure 22.2 The FORECAST Function Returning the Forecast of the Regression Line

F2 fx {=FORECAST(E2:E10,C2:C26,D2:D26)}

	A	B	C	D	E	F	G
1		ID	GPA (Y)	RANK (X)	New Rank	FORECAST (New Y)	
2		1	4.0	5	5	3.51	
3		2	3.2	4	4	3.20	
4		3	3.9	5	5	3.51	
5		4	2.7	3	3	2.89	
6		5	3.6	5	4	3.20	
7		6	1.9	1	5	3.51	
8		7	2.4	2	6	3.82	
9		8	3.6	4	5	3.51	
10		9	3.7	4	4	3.20	
11		10	3.2	2			
12		11	2.7	3			
13		12	2.1	1			
14		13	1.9	3			
15		14	1.7	3			
16		15	2.9	3			
17		16	3.1	2			
18		17	2.7	3			
19		18	3.6	4			
20		19	2.6	3			
21		20	3.1	4			
22		21	2.6	1			
23		22	2.9	1			
24		23	4.0	4			
25		24	3.8	3			
26		25	1.0	4			

Excel QuickGuide 23

The RSQ Function

What the RSQ Function Does

The RSQ function computes the square of the product-moment correlation between two variables.

The Data Set

The data set used in this example is titled RSQ, and the question is, "What is the RSQ, or the amount of variance accounted for, in the relationship between income and level of education?"

Variable	*Description*
Income	Annual income in dollars
Level of Education	Years of education as a percentile

Using the RSQ Function

1. **Click on the cell** where you want the RSQ function to be placed. (In the data set, the cell is C23.)
2. **Click Formulas → Insert Function** and you will see the Insert Function dialog box.
3. Locate and **double-click on the RSQ function** and you will see the Function Arguments dialog box as shown in Figure 23.1.
4. **Click the RefEdit button** in the Known_y's entry box and **drag the mouse** over the range of cells (D2 through D21) you want included in the analysis. **Click the RefEdit button.**
5. **Repeat Step 4** for Known_x's (Cells C2 through C21) and then **click the RefEdit button** and **click OK.** The RSQ function returns its value as .58 in Cell C23, as you see in Figure 23.2. You can see the syntax for the function in the formula bar at the top of the worksheet.

Related Functions: COVAR, CORREL, PEARSON, INTERCEPT, SLOPE, TREND, FORECAST

Figure 23.1 The RSQ Function Arguments Dialog Box

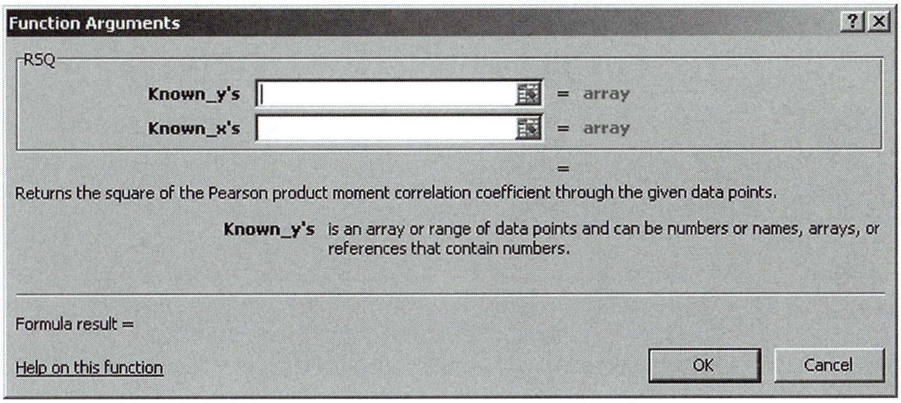

Function Arguments

RSQ

Known_y's = array

Known_x's = array

=

Returns the square of the Pearson product moment correlation coefficient through the given data points.

Known_y's is an array or range of data points and can be numbers or names, arrays, or references that contain numbers.

Formula result =

Help on this function

OK Cancel

Figure 23.2 The RSQ Function Returning the Squared Correlation

C23 fx =RSQ(D2:D21,C2:C21)

	A	B	C	D	E
1		ID	Income (X)	Level of Education (Y)	
2		1	$ 59,602	9	
3		2	$ 57,108	9	
4		3	$ 42,027	6	
5		4	$ 58,404	7	
6		5	$ 50,731	6	
7		6	$ 34,054	8	
8		7	$ 51,579	9	
9		8	$ 30,445	3	
10		9	$ 35,052	2	
11		10	$ 35,976	4	
12		11	$ 57,250	10	
13		12	$ 37,526	4	
14		13	$ 39,274	2	
15		14	$ 55,613	9	
16		15	$ 46,775	7	
17		16	$ 30,552	5	
18		17	$ 51,331	9	
19		18	$ 54,391	8	
20		19	$ 36,178	1	
21		20	$ 41,616	2	
22					
23		RSQ	0.58		
24					

Excel QuickGuide 24

The CHIDIST Function

What the CHIDIST Function Does

The CHIDIST function computes the probability of a value associated with a chi-square (χ^2) value. Use the CHITEST function for computing the χ^2 value.

The Data Set

The data set is titled CHIDIST and consists of the following variables. The question being asked is, "What is the probability of a type I error or alpha level associated with a chi square of .29?"

Variable	*Value*
Chi Square Value	Value of chi square
Degrees of Freedom	Degrees of freedom associated with the original chi-square analysis

Using the CHIDIST Function

1. **Click on the cell** where you want the CHIDIST function to be placed. (In the data set, the cell is C4.)
2. **Click Formulas → Insert Function** and you will see the Insert Function dialog box.
3. Locate and **double-click on the CHIDIST function** and you will see the Function Arguments dialog box as shown in Figure 24.1.
4. **Click the RefEdit button** in the X entry box and enter the chi-square value. In this example, it is Cell C1. **Click the RefEdit button.**
5. **Click the RefEdit button** in the Deg_Freedom entry box and click on the cell (C2) indicating the degrees of freedom.
6. **Click the RefEdit button** and press the return key or **click OK**. The CHIDIST function returns its value of .87 in Cell C4, as you see in Figure 24.2, indicating that it is highly likely that this value occurred by chance. Note that you can see the syntax for the function in the formula bar at the top of the worksheet.

Related Functions: CHITEST

Figure 24.1 The CHIDIST Function Arguments Dialog Box

Function Arguments

CHIDIST

X = number

Deg_freedom = number

=

This function is available for compatibility with Excel 2007 and earlier.
Returns the right-tailed probability of the chi-squared distribution.

X is the value at which you want to evaluate the distribution, a nonnegative number.

Formula result =

Help on this function

OK Cancel

Figure 24.2 The CHIDIST Function Returning the Probability Associated With a Chi-Square Value

C4 f_x =CHIDIST(C1,C2)

	A	B	C	D
1		Chi Square Value	0.29	
2		Degrees of Freedom	2	
3				
4		CHIDIST	0.87	

Excel QuickGuide 25

The CHITEST Function

What the CHITEST Function Does

The CHITEST function computes the chi square (χ^2) value for a test of independence for a nominal or categorical variable.

The Data Set

The data set used in this example is titled CHITEST, and the question is, "Are the actual and expected values for party affiliation independent of one another?"

Variable	*Description*
Party Affiliation	Frequency of actual and expected values for Democratic, Republican, and independent voters

Using the CHITEST Function

1. **Click on the cell** where you want the CHITEST function returned. (In the data set, the cell is B10.)
2. **Click Formulas → Insert Function** and you will see the Insert Function dialog box.
3. Locate and **double-click on the CHITEST function** and you will see the Function Arguments dialog box as shown in Figure 25.1.
4. **Click the RefEdit button** in the Actual_range entry box and **drag the mouse** over the range of cells (B8 through D8) you want included in the analysis. **Click the RefEdit button**.
5. **Click the RefEdit button** in the Expected_range entry box and **drag the mouse** over the range of cells (B4 through D4) you want included in the analysis.
6. **Click the RefEdit button** or press the return key and then **click OK**. The CHITEST function returns its value of .29 in Cell B10, as you see in Figure 25.2. Note that you can see the syntax for the function in the formula bar at the top of the worksheet.

Related Functions: CHIDIST

Figure 25.1 The CHITEST Function Arguments Dialog Box

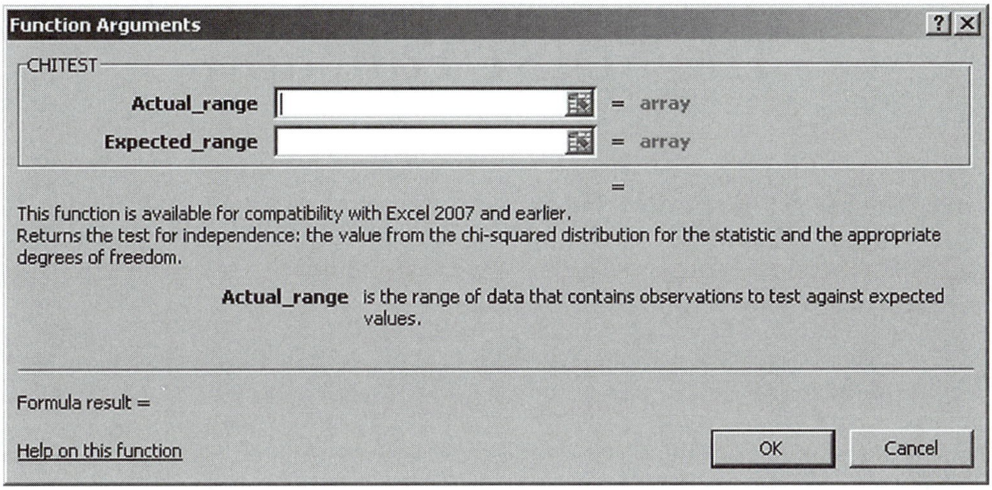

Function Arguments

CHITEST

Actual_range = array

Expected_range = array

=

This function is available for compatibility with Excel 2007 and earlier.
Returns the test for independence: the value from the chi-squared distribution for the statistic and the appropriate degrees of freedom.

Actual_range is the range of data that contains observations to test against expected values.

Formula result =

Help on this function

OK Cancel

Figure 25.2 The CHITEST Function Returning the Chi-Square (chi2) Value

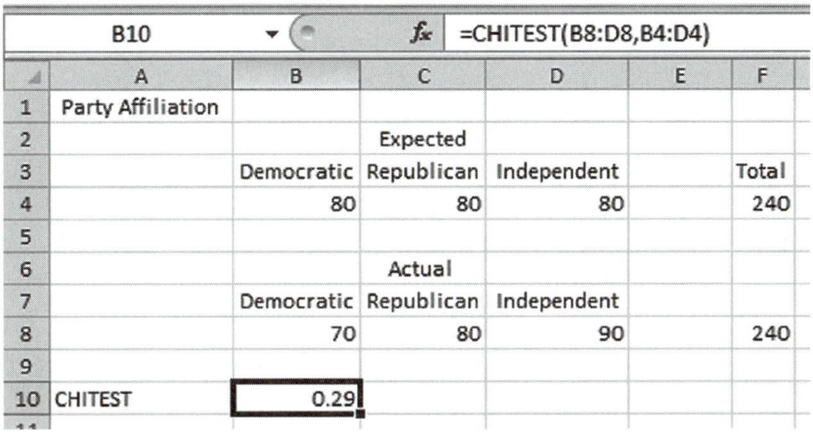

B10 fx =CHITEST(B8:D8,B4:D4)

	A	B	C	D	E	F
1	Party Affiliation					
2			Expected			
3		Democratic	Republican	Independent		Total
4		80	80	80		240
5						
6			Actual			
7		Democratic	Republican	Independent		
8		70	80	90		240
9						
10	CHITEST	0.29				

Excel QuickGuide 26

The FDIST Function

What the FDIST Function Does

The FDIST function computes the probability of a value associated with an *F* value. Use the FTEST function for computing the *F* value.

The Data Set

The data set is titled FDIST and consists of the following variables. The question being asked is, "What is the probability of a type I error or alpha level associated with an *F* value of 1.79 with 2 and 35 degrees of freedom?"

Variable	*Value*
F	Value of chi square
Degrees of Freedom (Numerator)	Degrees of freedom associated with the numerator
Degrees of Freedom (Denominator)	Degrees of freedom associated with the denominator

Using the FDIST Function

1. **Click on the cell** where you want the FDIST function to be placed. (In the data set, the cell is C5.)
2. **Click Formulas → Insert Function** and you will see the Insert Function dialog box.
3. Locate and **double-click on the FDIST function** and you will see the Function Arguments dialog box as shown in Figure 26.1.
4. **Click the RefEdit button** in the X entry box, enter the *F* value (Cell C1), and **click the RefEdit button**.
5. Repeat Step 4 for the Deg_freedom1 (Cell C2) and Deg_freedom2 (Cell C3).
6. **Click the RefEdit button** and **click OK**. The FDIST function returns its value of .18 in Cell C5, representing an insignificant probability for this *F* value, as you see in Figure 26.2. Note that you can see the syntax for the function in the formula bar at the top of the worksheet.

Related Functions: FTEST, TDIST, TTEST, ZTEST

Figure 26.1 The FDIST Function Arguments Dialog Box

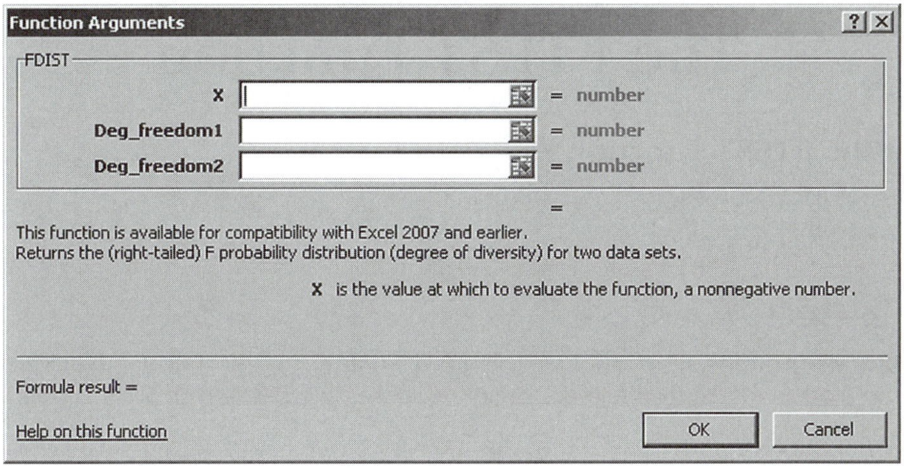

Function Arguments

FDIST

X = number

Deg_freedom1 = number

Deg_freedom2 = number

=

This function is available for compatibility with Excel 2007 and earlier.
Returns the (right-tailed) F probability distribution (degree of diversity) for two data sets.

X is the value at which to evaluate the function, a nonnegative number.

Formula result =

Help on this function

OK Cancel

Figure 26.2 The FDIST Function Returning the Probability Associated With an F Value

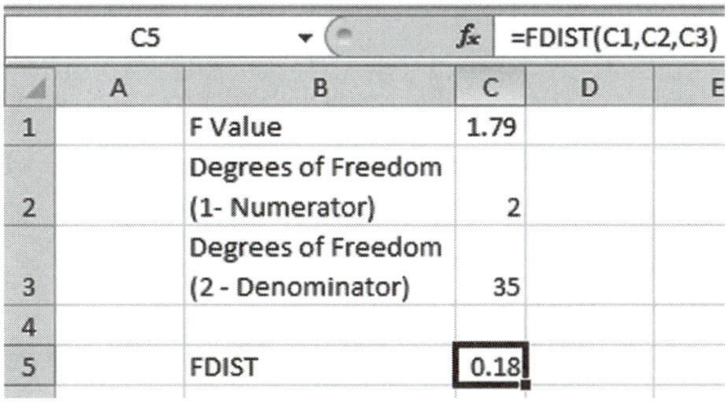

C5 =FDIST(C1,C2,C3)

	A	B	C	D	E
1		F Value	1.79		
2		Degrees of Freedom (1- Numerator)	2		
3		Degrees of Freedom (2 - Denominator)	35		
4					
5		FDIST	0.18		

Excel QuickGuide 27

The FTEST Function

What the FTEST Function Does

The FTEST function computes the probability that the associated *F* value is not significantly different from zero.

The Data Set

The data set used in this example is titled FTEST, and the question is, "Does studying using an iPod significantly affect the final test score of two different groups of first-year college students?"

Variable	*Description*
iPod	Final test score with the help program
No iPod	Final test score without the help program

Using the FTEST Function

To use the FTEST function, follow these steps:

1. **Click on the cell** where you want the FTEST function returned. (In the data set, the cell is C23.)
2. **Click Formulas → Insert Function** and you will see the Insert Function dialog box.
3. Locate and **double-click on the FTEST function** and you will see the Function Arguments dialog box as shown in Figure 27.1.
4. **Click the RefEdit button** in the Array1 entry box.
5. **Drag the mouse** over the range of cells (C2 through C21) you want included in the analysis and **click the RefEdit button**.
6. **Click the RefEdit button** in the Array2 entry box.
7. **Drag the mouse** over the range of cells (D2 through D21) you want included in the analysis and **click the RefEdit button**.
8. **Click the RefEdit button** and **click OK**. The FTEST function returns its value of .12 in Cell C23, as you see in Figure 27.2, indicating that the difference between groups on final test score is not significant at the .05 level. Note that you can see the syntax for the function in the formula bar at the top of the worksheet.

Related Functions: FDIST, TDIST, TTEST, ZTEST

Figure 27.1 The FTEST Function Arguments Dialog Box

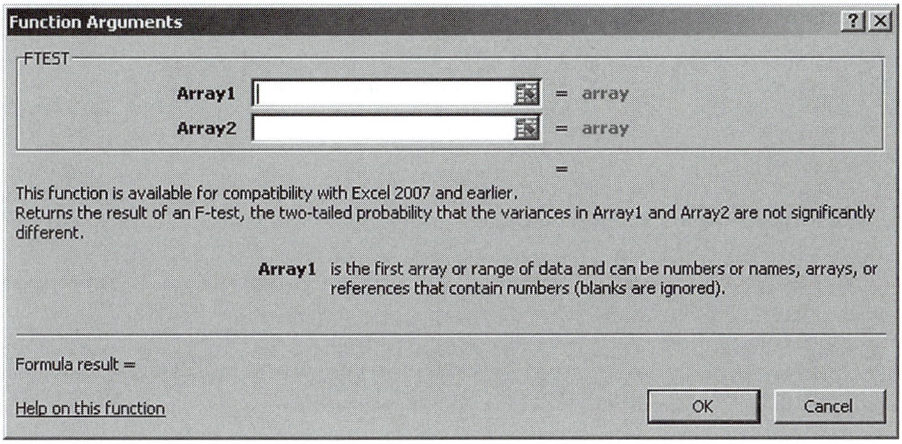

Function Arguments

FTEST

Array1 = array

Array2 = array

=

This function is available for compatibility with Excel 2007 and earlier.
Returns the result of an F-test, the two-tailed probability that the variances in Array1 and Array2 are not significantly different.

Array1 is the first array or range of data and can be numbers or names, arrays, or references that contain numbers (blanks are ignored).

Formula result =

Help on this function

OK Cancel

Figure 27.2 The FTEST Function Returning the Probability of the *F* Value

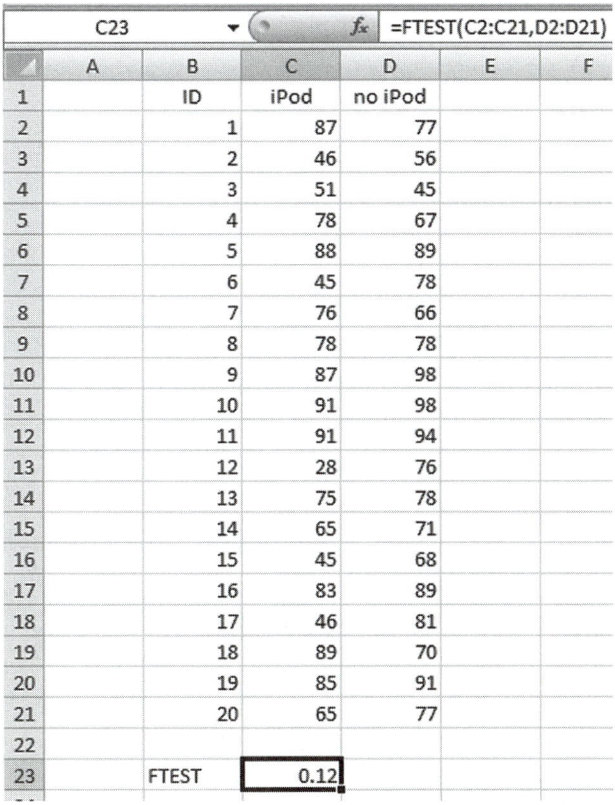

C23 f_x =FTEST(C2:C21,D2:D21)

	A	B	C	D	E	F
1		ID	iPod	no iPod		
2		1	87	77		
3		2	46	56		
4		3	51	45		
5		4	78	67		
6		5	88	89		
7		6	45	78		
8		7	76	66		
9		8	78	78		
10		9	87	98		
11		10	91	98		
12		11	91	94		
13		12	28	76		
14		13	75	78		
15		14	65	71		
16		15	45	68		
17		16	83	89		
18		17	46	81		
19		18	89	70		
20		19	85	91		
21		20	65	77		
22						
23		FTEST	0.12			

Excel QuickGuide 28

The TDIST Function

What the TDIST Function Does

The TDIST function computes the probability of a value associated with the student's *t* value. Use the TTEST function for computing the *t* value.

The Data Set

The data set is titled TDIST and consists of the following variables. The question being asked is, "What is the probability of a type I error or alpha level associated with a one-tailed test and a *t* value of 1.96 with 50 degrees of freedom?"

Variable	*Value*
X	Value of *t*
Degrees of Freedom	Degrees of freedom
Tails	1 = one-tailed test, 2 = two-tailed test

Using the TDIST Function

1. **Click on the cell** where you want the TDIST function to be placed. (In the data set, the cell is C5.)
2. **Click Formulas → Insert Function** and you will see the Insert Function dialog box.
3. Locate and **double-click on the TDIST function** and you will see the Function Arguments dialog box as shown in Figure 28.1.
4. **Click the RefEdit button** in the X entry box and enter the *t* value. In this example, it is Cell C1. **Click the RefEdit button.**
5. **Repeat Step 4** for the Deg_freedom entry box and enter the degrees of freedom value (Cell C2) and the Tails entry box (Cell C3). **Click the RefEdit button.**
6. **Click the RefEdit button** and **click OK**. The TDIST function returns its value of .028 in Cell C5, as you see in Figure 28.2, indicating that the *t* value is significant beyond the .05 level. Note that you can see the syntax for the function in the formula bar at the top of the worksheet.

Related Functions: FDIST, FTEST, TTEST, ZTEST

Figure 28.1 The TDIST Function Arguments Dialog Box

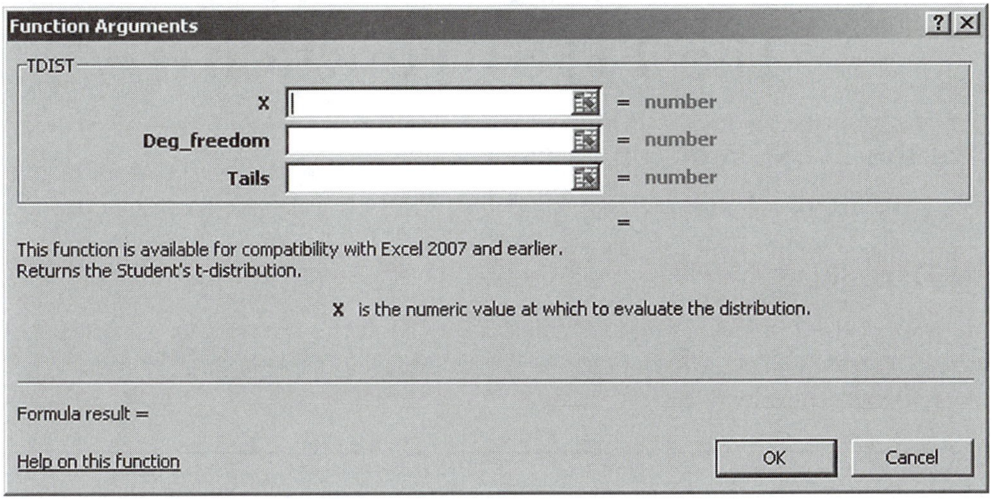

Function Arguments

TDIST

X = number

Deg_freedom = number

Tails = number

=

This function is available for compatibility with Excel 2007 and earlier.
Returns the Student's t-distribution.

X is the numeric value at which to evaluate the distribution.

Formula result =

Help on this function

OK Cancel

Figure 28.2 The TDIST Function Returning the Probability Associated With a *t* Value

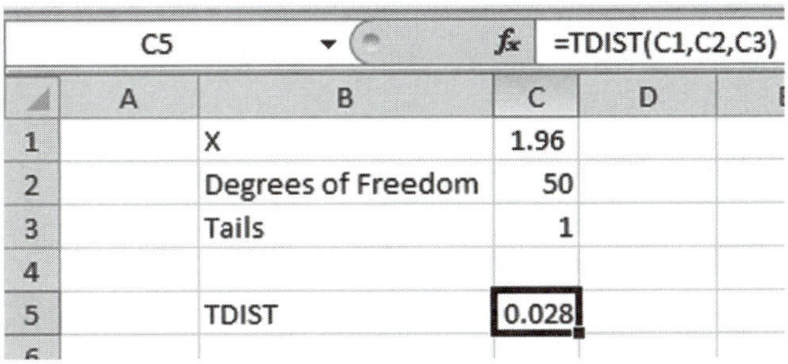

C5 =TDIST(C1,C2,C3)

	A	B	C	D
1		X	1.96	
2		Degrees of Freedom	50	
3		Tails	1	
4				
5		TDIST	0.028	

Excel QuickGuide 29

The TTEST Function

What the TTEST Function Does

The TTEST function computes the probability of the associated Student's *t* value.

The Data Set

The data set used in this example is titled TTEST, and the question is, "Is there a significant difference in achievement scores between fall and spring testings for the same group of college students?"

Variable	*Description*
Fall	Fall test scores
Spring	Spring test scores

Using the TTEST Function

To use the TTEST function, follow these steps:

1. **Click on the cell** where you want the TTEST function returned. (In the data set, the cell is C23.)
2. **Click Formulas → Insert Function** and you will see the Insert Function dialog box.
3. Locate and **double-click on the TTEST function** and you will see the Function Arguments dialog box as shown in Figure 29.1.
4. **Click the RefEdit button** in the Array1 entry box.
5. **Drag the mouse** over the range of cells (C2 through C21) you want included in the analysis and **click the RefEdit button**.
6. **Click the RefEdit button** in the Array2 entry box.
7. **Drag the mouse** over the range of cells (D2 through D21) you want included in the analysis and **click the RefEdit button**.
8. In the Tails entry box, **enter the value 2** and in the Type entry box, **enter the value 1** (for a paired *t*-test).
9. **Click OK**. The TTEST function returns its value of .14 in Cell C23, as you see in Figure 29.2, indicating that the probability of the associated *t* value occurring by

chance alone is .14. Note that you can see the syntax for the function in the formula bar at the top of the worksheet.

Related Functions: FDIST, FTEST, TDIST, ZTEST

Figure 29.1 The TTEST Function Arguments Dialog Box

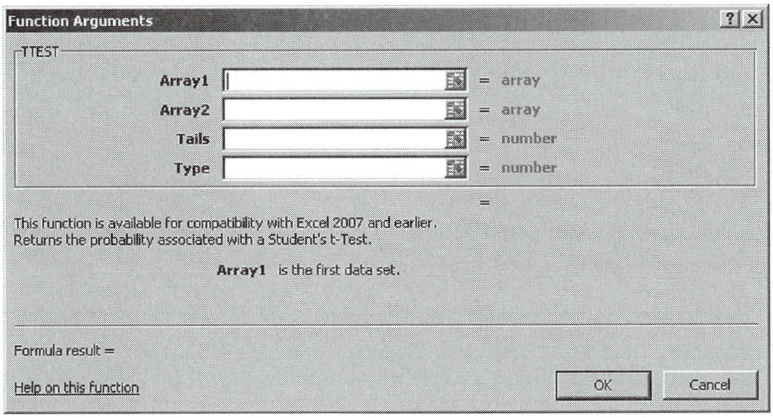

Function Arguments

TTEST

Array1 = array
Array2 = array
Tails = number
Type = number

=

This function is available for compatibility with Excel 2007 and earlier.
Returns the probability associated with a Student's t-Test.

Array1 is the first data set.

Formula result =

Help on this function

OK Cancel

Figure 29.2 The TTEST Function Returning the Probability of the Student's *t* Value

C23 *fx* =TTEST(C2:C21,D2:D21,2,1)

	A	B	C	D	E
1		ID	Fall	Spring	
2		6	5	4	
3		2	5	5	
4		3	4	4	
5		4	7	3	
6		5	8	3	
7		6	7	8	
8		7	6	7	
9		8	3	6	
10		9	6	5	
11		10	2	6	
12		11	6	9	
13		12	4	8	
14		13	5	9	
15		14	7	8	
16		15	8	9	
17		16	7	8	
18		17	5	9	
19		18	9	8	
20		19	8	9	
21		20	6	7	
22					
23		TTEST	0.14		

Excel QuickGuide 30

The ZTEST Function

What the ZTEST Function Does

The ZTEST function computes the probability that a single score belongs to a population of scores.

The Data Set

The data set used in this example is titled ZTEST, and the question is, "Does a score of 82 belong to the population set of scores?"

Variable	*Description*
MEMO	Score on a recall memory test ranging from 1 to 100
X	The score to be tested
Sigma	The population standard deviation (computed using the STDEVP function)

Using the ZTEST Function

To use the ZTEST function, follow these steps:

1. **Click on the cell** where you want the ZTEST function returned. (In the data set, the cell is C18.)
2. **Click Formulas → Insert Function** and you will see the Insert Function dialog box.
3. Locate and **double-click on the ZTEST function** and you will see the Function Arguments dialog box as shown in Figure 30.1.
4. **Click the RefEdit button** in the Array entry box.
5. **Drag the mouse** over the range of cells (C2 through C16) you want included in the analysis and **click the RefEdit button.**
6. **Click the RefEdit button** in the X entry box.
7. **Click on the X value** for which you want to compute the Z test (Cell D2) and **click the RefEdit button.**
8. **Click the RefEdit button** and click on the population standard deviation (Cell E2) and **click the RefEdit button.**
9. **Click OK.** The ZTEST function returns its value of .94 in Cell C18, as you see in Figure 30.2, indicating that it is highly likely the X value belongs to the set of

sample scores and is not unique. Note that you can see the syntax for the function in the formula bar at the top of the worksheet.

Related Functions: FDIST, FTEST, TDIST, TTEST

Figure 30.1 The ZTEST Function Arguments Dialog Box

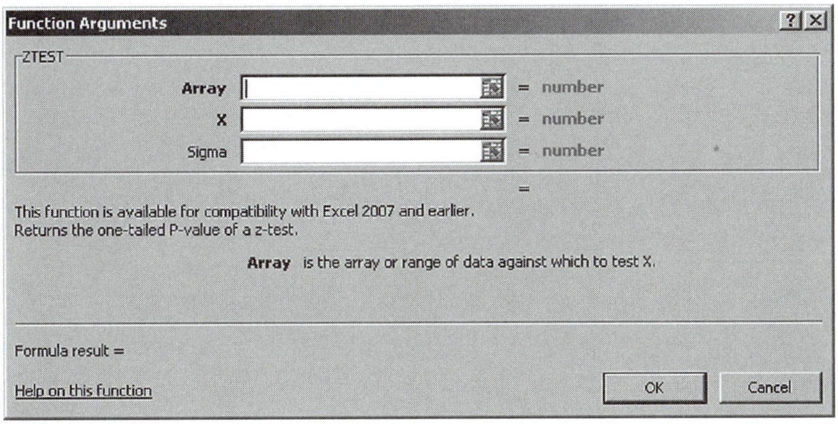

Function Arguments

ZTEST

Array = number

X = number

Sigma = number

=

This function is available for compatibility with Excel 2007 and earlier.
Returns the one-tailed P-value of a z-test.

Array is the array or range of data against which to test X.

Formula result =

Help on this function

OK Cancel

Figure 30.2 The ZTEST Function Returning the Probability of a Single Value

C18 =ZTEST(C2:C16,D2,E2)

	A	B	C	D	E
1		ID	MEMO	X	Sigma
2		1	67	82	11.44
3		2	67		
4		3	87		
5		4	89		
6		5	87		
7		6	77		
8		7	73		
9		8	74		
10		9	68		
11		10	72		
12		11	58		
13		12	98		
14		13	98		
15		14	70		
16		15	77		
17					
18		ZTEST	0.94		

PART II

USING THE ANALYSIS TOOLPAK

The Excel Analysis ToolPak is a set of automated tools that allows you to conduct a variety of simple and complex statistical analyses. They are similar to Excel functions in that each requires input from the user, but they produce much more elaborate output rather than just one outcome (as do most functions).

For example, the Descriptive Statistics tool in the Analysis ToolPak produces the mean, median, and mode, among other descriptive measures. To compute such values using functions, you would have to use at least three different functions. Here, you can do it (and more) by using only one.

The basic method for using any one of the ToolPak tools is as follows:

1. From the Data tab, select the Data Analysis option.
2. Select the tool you want to use.
3. Enter the data and the type of the analysis you want done.
4. Format the data as you see fit. In the examples used in this part of *Excel Statistics: A Quick Guide,* the data may have been reformatted to appear more pleasing to the eye and to be more internally consistent (for example, numbers are formatted to two decimal places, labels may be centered when appropriate, etc.).

The process is very much like using a function, including use of the RefEdit button to enter data into the dialog box, but there are also a number of decisions you may have to make as you prepare the analysis.

Among these are the following:

1. If you want labels to be used in the ToolPak output
2. Whether you want the output to appear on the current Excel worksheet, on a new worksheet, or in an entirely new workbook
3. Whether the results should be grouped by columns or rows
4. The range of cells in which you want the output to appear
5. Whether you have to enter data in the Data Analysis dialog box rather than using the RefEdit button and dragging over the data

For the purposes of our illustrations, we are always going to use labels, will have the output appear on the same worksheet, and will group the output by columns. The range of cells in which the output should appear will be defined as each Analysis ToolPak tool is discussed. And, the final or partial output you see will always be reformatted to better fit the page.

Once the Analysis ToolPak output is complete, it can be manipulated as any Excel data can. In addition to cutting and pasting into other applications such as Word, the output can easily be modified using Excel's Format as Table option on the Home tab. For example, the simple output you see in Figure 17.2 can easily be reformatted to appear as shown in Figure B1.

Figure B1 Modifying Excel Analysis ToolPak Output

ID	Height	Weight
1	60	134
2	63	143
3	71	156
4	58	121
5	61	131
6	59	117
7	64	125
8	67	126
9	63	143
10	52	98
11	61	154
12	58	125
13	54	109
14	61	117
15	64	126
16	63	154
17	49	98
18	59	143
19	69	144
20	71	156
CORREL	0.78	

Excel QuickGuide 31

Descriptive Statistics

What the Descriptive Statistics Tool Does

The Descriptive Statistics tool computes basic descriptive statistics for a set of data, such as the mean, median, and mode, among several others.

The Data Set

The data set used in this example is titled DESCRIPTIVE STATISTICS, and the question is, "What are the descriptive statistics for height for a group of 20 two-year-olds?"

Variable	*Description*
Height	Height in inches

Using the Descriptive Statistics Tool

1. **Select the Data Analysis option** from the Data tab.
2. **Double-click on the Descriptive Statistics option** in the Data Analysis dialog box and you will see the Descriptive Statistics dialog box shown in Figure 31.1.
3. Define the Input Range by **clicking on the RefEdit button** and selecting the data you want to use in the analysis (in this example, Cells B2 through B21), and **click the RefEdit button** once again. Be sure to check the Labels in First Row box.
4. **Click the Output Range button** and define the Output Range by selecting an area in the worksheet where you want the output to appear (in this example, Cell D2) and **click the RefEdit button** once again. Even though the range is only one cell, Excel will know to extend it to fit all the output.
5. Click the **Summary Statistics option** and **click OK.**

The Final Output

The Descriptive Statistics output is shown in Figure 31.2, including the original data and the summary statistics. Note that the cells were formatted where appropriate using the Format Cells command. Otherwise, Excel produced what you see as the final output.

Figure 31.1 The Descriptive Statistics Dialog Box

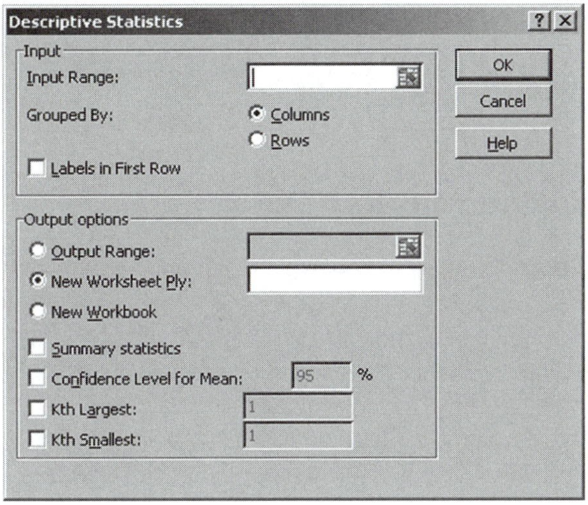

Descriptive Statistics

Input
Input Range:
Grouped By: Columns / Rows
Labels in First Row

OK
Cancel
Help

Output options
Output Range:
New Worksheet Ply:
New Workbook
Summary statistics
Confidence Level for Mean: 95 %
Kth Largest: 1
Kth Smallest: 1

Figure 31.2 The Descriptive Statistics Output

	A	B	C	D	E
1		Height			
2		38		*Height*	
3		28			
4		28		Mean	32.70
5		40		Standard Error	1.04
6		29		Median	33.50
7		36		Mode	28.00
8		35		Standard Deviation	4.64
9		28		Sample Variance	21.48
10		38		Kurtosis	-1.35
11		37		Skewness	0.08
12		35		Range	14.00
13		34		Minimum	26.00
14		26		Maximum	40.00
15		26		Sum	654.00
16		40		Count	20
17		31			
18		30			
19		34			
20		33			
21		28			

Excel QuickGuide 32

Moving Average

What the Moving Average Tool Does

The Moving Average tool computes the average for sets of numbers of a defined interval.

The Data Set

The data set used in this example is titled MOVING AVERAGE, and the question is, "What is the moving average for subsequent 4-week periods for number of home sales?"

Variable	*Description*
Sales	Number of home sales in a 1-week period

Using the Moving Average Tool

1. **Select the Data Analysis option** from the Data tab.
2. **Double click on the Moving Average option** in the Data Analysis dialog box and you will see the Moving Average dialog box shown in Figure 32.1.
3. Define the Input Range by **clicking on the RefEdit button** and selecting the data you want to use in the analysis (in this example, C2 through C13), and **clicking the RefEdit button** once again. Be sure to check the Labels in First Row box.
4. Define the interval or the number of values you want to form each average (in this example, it is 4 entered directly in the dialog box).
5. **Click the Output Range button** and define the Output Range by selecting an area in the worksheet where you want the output to appear (in this example, E2) and **click the RefEdit button** once again. Even though the range is only one cell, Excel will know to extend it to fit all the output.
6. **Click the Chart Output check box** and **click OK.**

The Final Output

The Moving Average output is shown in Figure 32.2, including the original data and the averages. As you can see, the first three averages are marked #N/A because Excel must detect four averages before it can compute the first one. Otherwise, Excel produced what you see as the final output, including a chart.

Figure 32.1 The Moving Average Dialog Box

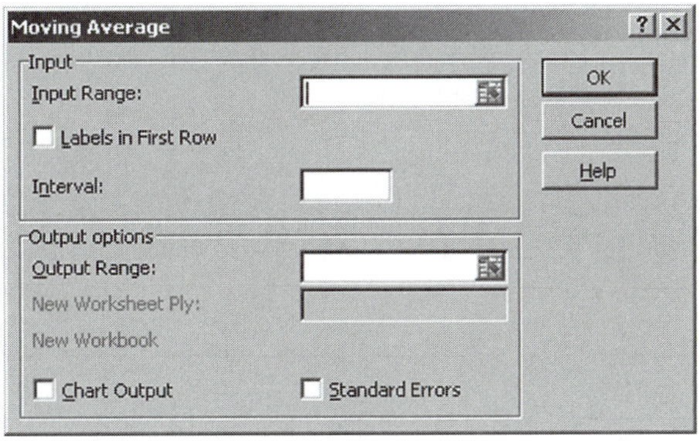

Figure 32.2 The Moving Average Output

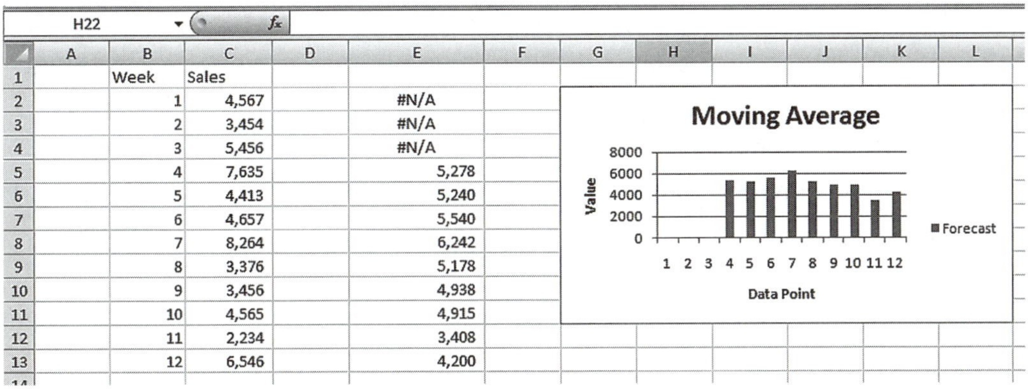

	A	B	C	D	E
1		Week	Sales		
2		1	4,567		#N/A
3		2	3,454		#N/A
4		3	5,456		#N/A
5		4	7,635		5,278
6		5	4,413		5,240
7		6	4,657		5,540
8		7	8,264		6,242
9		8	3,376		5,178
10		9	3,456		4,938
11		10	4,565		4,915
12		11	2,234		3,408
13		12	6,546		4,200

Excel QuickGuide 33

Random Number Generation

What the Random Number Generation Tool Does

The Random Number Generation tool produces a set of random numbers.

The Data Set

The data set used in this example is titled RANDOM NUMBER GENERATOR, and the tool generates a random number for each of the 20 members of the group that will be used in the assignment of members to experimental (odd number) or control (even number) groups.

Variable	*Description*
ID	Participant's identifying number
Random Number	Random number assigned to each ID

Using the Random Number Generation Tool

1. **Select the Data Analysis option** from the Data tab.
2. **Double click on the Random Number Generation** option in the Data Analysis dialog box and you will see the Random Number Generation dialog box shown in Figure 33.1.
3. **Define the Number of Variables** (in this example, it was 1).
4. **Define the Number of Random Numbers** (in this example, it was 20).
5. **Select Normal** from the Distribution drop-down menu.
6. **Enter 1** for Mean.
7. **Enter 1** for Standard deviation.
8. **Click on the RefEdit button** for the Output Range and select the range where you want the random numbers to be placed (in this example, it is C2 through C21).
9. **Click the RefEdit button** and **click OK.**

The Final Output

The 20 random digits appear as shown in Figure 33.2. Numbers ending in an odd digit are to be placed in the experimental group, and numbers ending in an even digit are placed in the control group.

Figure 33.1 The Random Number Generation Dialog Box

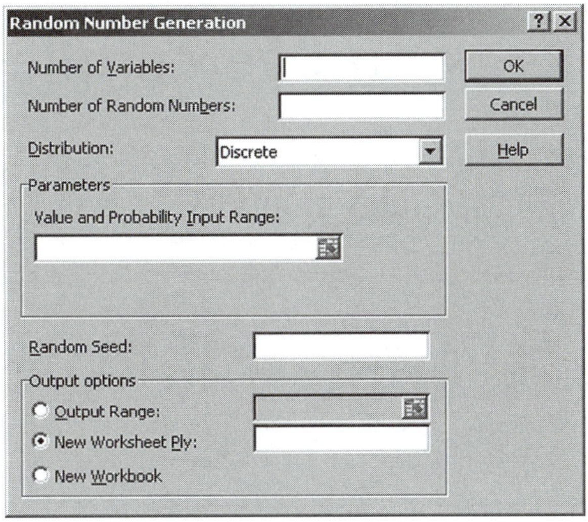

Random Number Generation

Number of Variables:

Number of Random Numbers:

Distribution: Discrete

Parameters

Value and Probability Input Range:

Random Seed:

Output options

Output Range:

New Worksheet Ply:

New Workbook

OK

Cancel

Help

Figure 33.2 The Random Number Generation Output

O23

	A	B	C
1		ID	RANDOM NUMBERS
2		1	-0.0934
3		2	0.6544
4		3	1.0677
5		4	-1.6201
6		5	1.4727
7		6	1.9015
8		7	2.4464
9		8	1.0445
10		9	-0.2881
11		10	0.8237
12		11	0.4194
13		12	0.9804
14		13	0.0769
15		14	1.9462
16		15	0.3364
17		16	2.0720
18		17	2.1668
19		18	0.6973
20		19	0.9630
21		20	2.4671

Excel QuickGuide 34

Rank and Percentile

What the Rank and Percentile Tool Does

The Rank and Percentile tool produces the point, rank, and percentiles for a set of scores.

The Data Set

The data set used in this example is titled RANK AND PERCENTILE, and the question is, "What are the rank and percentile scores for a set of 10 grade point averages (GPAs)?"

Variable	*Description*
GPA	Grade point average

Using the Rank and Percentile Tool

1. **Select the Data Analysis option** from the Data tab.
2. **Double-click on the Rank and Percentile option** in the Data Analysis dialog box and you will see the Rank and Percentile dialog box shown in Figure 34.1.
3. Be sure that the Columns button and the Labels in First Row checkbox are selected.
4. **Click the RefEdit button** in the Input Range and select the data you want to use in the analysis (in this example, it is B1 through B11). **Click the RefEdit button** again.
5. **Click the RefEdit button** in the Output Range and select the location where you want the output to appear (in this example, it is D1). **Click the RefEdit button** again.
6. **Click OK.**

The Final Output

The point (the physical location in the original set of data), the GPA, the rank, and the percent (percentile) are shown in Figure 34.2.

Figure 34.1 The Rank and Percentile Dialog Box

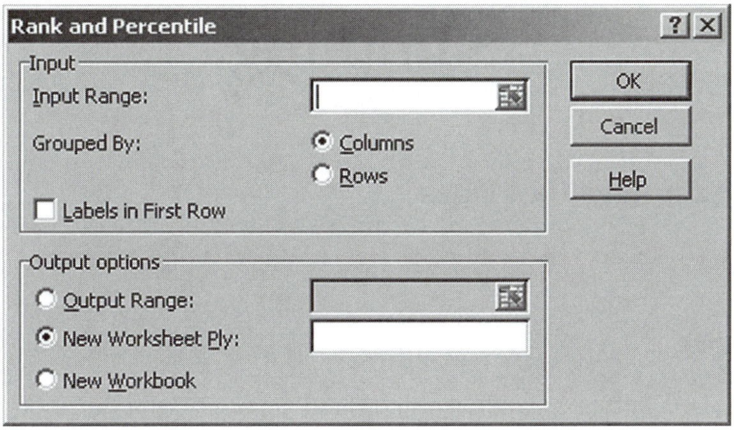

Rank and Percentile

Input

Input Range:

Grouped By: Columns / Rows

Labels in First Row

OK

Cancel

Help

Output options

Output Range:

New Worksheet Ply:

New Workbook

Figure 34.2 The Rank and Percentile Output

	A	B	C	D	E	F	G
1		GPA		*Point*	*GPA*	*Rank*	*Percent*
2		3.8		6	3.9	1	100.00%
3		2.5		1	3.8	2	88.80%
4		3.1		9	3.5	3	77.70%
5		1.6		3	3.1	4	66.60%
6		2.8		5	2.8	5	55.50%
7		3.9		7	2.6	6	44.40%
8		2.6		2	2.5	7	33.30%
9		1.2		10	2.2	8	22.20%
10		3.5		4	1.6	9	11.10%
11		2.2		8	1.2	10	0.00%

Excel QuickGuide 35

Sampling

What the Sampling Tool Does

The Sampling tool produces a sample as selected from a population.

The Data Set

The data set used in this example is titled SAMPLING, and the question is, "What are the ID numbers of 10 participants selected at random from a population of 100?"

Variable	*Description*
ID	Identification number

Using the Sampling Tool

1. **Select the Data Analysis option** from the Data tab.
2. **Double-click on the Sampling option** in the Data Analysis dialog box and you will see the Sampling dialog box shown in Figure 35.1.
3. **Click the RefEdit button** in the Input Range entry box and select the data you want to use in the analysis (in this example, it is B2 through F21). **Click the RefEdit button** again.
4. **Click the Random button** and enter the number you want randomly selected. In this example, the number is 10.
5. **Click the RefEdit button** in the Output Range and select the location where you want the output to appear (in this example, it is H2 through H11). **Click the RefEdit button** again.
6. **Click OK**.

The Final Output

The 10 ID numbers randomly selected are shown in Figure 35.2.

Figure 35.1 The Sampling Dialog Box

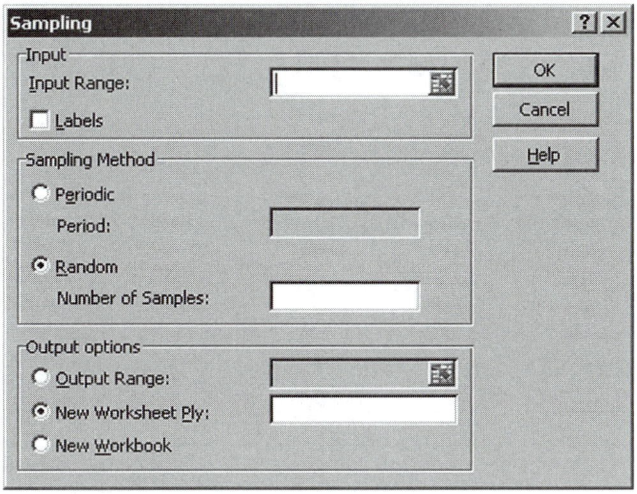

Sampling
Input
Input Range:
Labels
Sampling Method
Periodic
Period:
Random
Number of Samples:
Output options
Output Range:
New Worksheet Ply:
New Workbook
OK
Cancel
Help

Figure 35.2 The Sampling Output

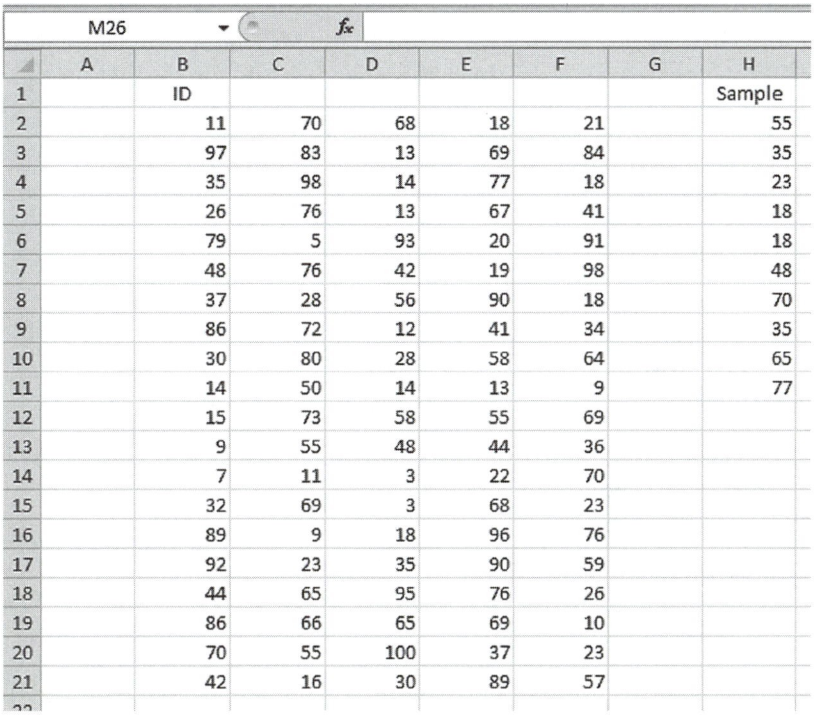

M26 fx

	A	B	C	D	E	F	G	H
1		ID						Sample
2		11	70	68	18	21		55
3		97	83	13	69	84		35
4		35	98	14	77	18		23
5		26	76	13	67	41		18
6		79	5	93	20	91		18
7		48	76	42	19	98		48
8		37	28	56	90	18		70
9		86	72	12	41	34		35
10		30	80	28	58	64		65
11		14	50	14	13	9		77
12		15	73	58	55	69		
13		9	55	48	44	36		
14		7	11	3	22	70		
15		32	69	3	68	23		
16		89	9	18	96	76		
17		92	23	35	90	59		
18		44	65	95	76	26		
19		86	66	65	69	10		
20		70	55	100	37	23		
21		42	16	30	89	57		

Excel QuickGuide 36

z-Test: Two-Sample for Means

What the z-Test: Two-Sample for Means Tool Does

The z-Test: Two-Sample for Means computes a *z* value between means when the population variances are known.

The Data Set

The data set used in this example is titled ZTEST, and the question is, "Do the population means for urban and rural residents differ on a test of energy use?"

Variable	*Description*
Energy Use	Total annual energy costs in dollars

Using the z-Test: Two-Sample for Means Tool

1. **Select the Data Analysis option** from the Data tab.
2. **Double-click** on the **z-Test: Two-Sample for Means option** in the Data Analysis dialog box and you will see the z-Test: Two-Sample for Means dialog box shown in Figure 36.1.
3. Be sure that the Labels box in the Input area is checked.
4. **Click the RefEdit button** in the Variable 1 Range entry box and select the data you want to use in the analysis. In this example, it is Cells B1 through B21. **Click the RefEdit button** again.
5. **Click the RefEdit button** in the Variable 2 Range entry box and select the data you want to use in the analysis. In this example, it is Cells C1 through C21. **Click the RefEdit button** again.
6. Enter what you expect the mean difference to be. In this example, we entered 1000.
7. Enter the known population variance for both arrays of data. In this example, VARP was used to compute these values and is available in Cells B23 and C23.
8. **Click the RefEdit button** and enter the output range. In this example, Cell E1 was selected. **Click the RefEdit button again** and **click OK.**

The Final Output

The results are shown in Figure 36.2 with a *z* value of 3.02, which is significant beyond the .05 level (as specified in the dialog box you see in Figure 36.1), indicating that urban and rural residents differ in their energy use.

Figure 36.1 The z-Test: Two-Sample for Means Dialog Box

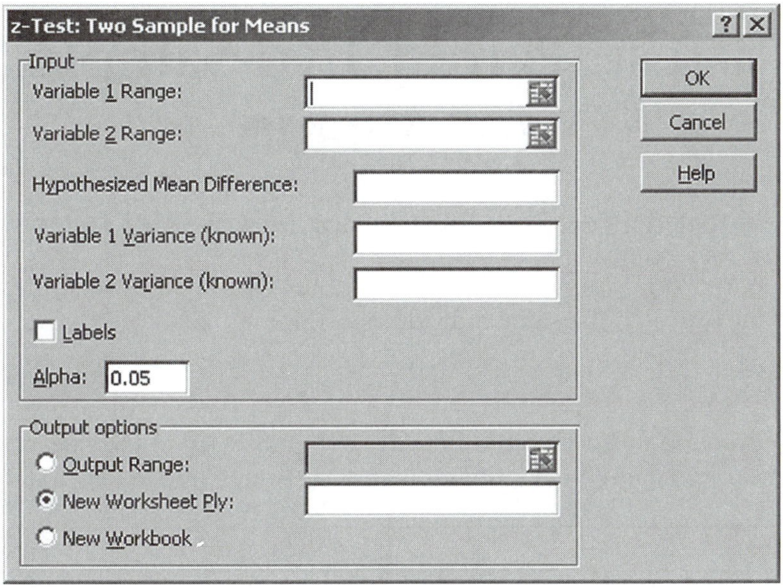

z-Test: Two Sample for Means

Input

Variable 1 Range:

Variable 2 Range:

Hypothesized Mean Difference:

Variable 1 Variance (known):

Variable 2 Variance (known):

Labels

Alpha: 0.05

Output options

Output Range:

New Worksheet Ply:

New Workbook

OK

Cancel

Help

Figure 36.2 The z-Test: Two-Sample for Means Output

F28

	A	B	C	D	E	F	G
1		Urban	Rural				
2		$ 4,534	$ 1,536		z-Test: Two Sample for Means		
3		$ 5,453	$ 3,344				
4		$ 6,567	$ 3,242			*Urban*	*Rural*
5		$ 6,534	$ 1,121		Mean	5417.2	2978.65
6		$ 1,545	$ 4,322		Known Variance	2770138.56	1766068.03
7		$ 6,634	$ 3,223		Observations	20	20
8		$ 7,645	$ 3,234		Hypothesized Mean Difference	1000	
9		$ 4,534	$ 1,212		z	3.02	
10		$ 5,665	$ 5,434		P(Z<=z) one-tail	0.001	
11		$ 6,765	$ 987		z Critical one-tail	1.64	
12		$ 6,653	$ 4,531		P(Z<=z) two-tail	0.00	
13		$ 2,546	$ 2,321		z Critical two-tail	1.96	
14		$ 5,434	$ 4,332				
15		$ 8,765	$ 3,323				
16		$ 6,536	$ 2,323				
17		$ 3,657	$ 4,323				
18		$ 4,366	$ 776				
19		$ 5,421	$ 3,211				
20		$ 4,567	$ 2,324				
21		$ 4,523	$ 4,454				
22							
23	VARP	$ 2,770,138.56	$ 1,766,068.03				

Excel QuickGuide 37

t-Test: Paired Two-Sample for Means

What the t-Test: Paired Two-Sample for Means Tool Does

The t-Test: Paired Two-Sample for Means computes a *t* value between means for two dependent measures on the same individuals or case.

The Data Set

The data set used in this example is titled TTEST–PAIRED, and the question is, "Does an intervention program reduce the number of cigarettes smoked each day?"

Variable	*Description*
Before	Number of cigarettes smoked before the intervention
After	Number of cigarettes smoked after the intervention

Using the t-Test: Paired Two-Sample for Means Tool

1. **Select the Data Analysis option** from the Data tab.
2. **Double-click** on the **t-Test: Paired Two-Sample for Means option** in the Data Analysis dialog box and you will see the t-Test: Paired Two-Sample for Means dialog box shown in Figure 37.1.
3. Be sure that the Labels box in the Input area is checked.
4. **Click the RefEdit button** in the Variable 1 Range entry box and select the data you want to use in the analysis. In this example, it is Cells B1 through B21. **Click the RefEdit button again.**
5. **Click the RefEdit button** in the Variable 2 Range entry box and select the data you want to use in the analysis. In this example, it is Cells C1 through C21. **Click the RefEdit button again.**
6. **Click the RefEdit button** and enter the output range. In this example, Cell E1 is selected. **Click the RefEdit button again** and **click OK.**

The Final Output

The results are shown in Figure 37.2 with a *t* value of 1.58, which is not significant beyond the .05 level (as specified in the dialog box you see in Figure 37.1), indicating that the intervention was not effective and there was no difference in rate of daily cigarette smoking.

Figure 37.1 The t-Test: Paired Two-Sample for Means Dialog Box

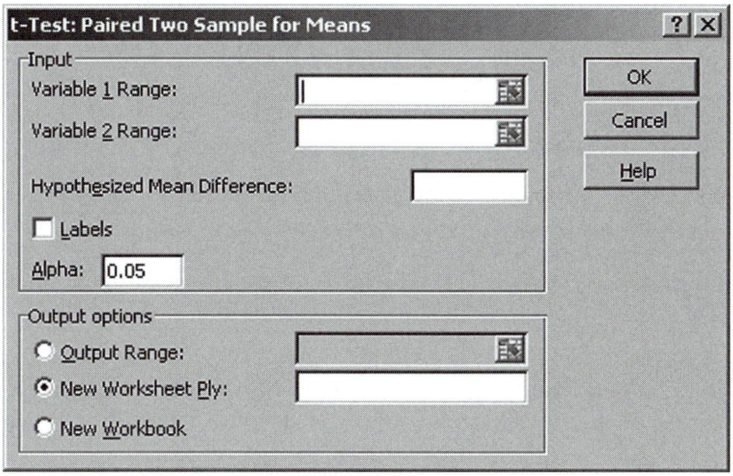

t-Test: Paired Two Sample for Means

Input

Variable 1 Range:

Variable 2 Range:

Hypothesized Mean Difference:

Labels

Alpha: 0.05

Output options

Output Range:

New Worksheet Ply:

New Workbook

OK

Cancel

Help

Figure 37.2 The t-Test: Paired Two-Sample for Means Output

N30 fx

	A	B	C	D	E	F	G
1		Before	After				
2		20	19		t-Test: Paired Two Sample for Means		
3		34	17				
4		18	23			*Before*	*After*
5		16	14		Mean	25.05	22.7
6		13	16		Variance	66.58	48.85
7		32	32		Observations	20	20
8		36	28		Pearson Correlation	0.62	
9		38	26		Hypothesized Mean Difference	0	
10		26	27		df	19	
11		33	37		t Stat	1.58	
12		31	28		P(T<=t) one-tail	0.07	
13		21	20		t Critical one-tail	1.73	
14		15	17		P(T<=t) two-tail	0.13	
15		17	14		t Critical two-tail	2.09	
16		18	16				
17		29	22				
18		15	24				
19		33	36				
20		25	22				
21		31	16				

Excel QuickGuide 38

t-Test: Two-Sample Assuming Unequal Variances

What the t-Test: Two-Sample Assuming Unequal Variances Tool Does

The t-Test: Two-Sample for Means computes a *t* value between means for two independent measures when the variances for each group are unequal.

The Data Set

The data set used in this example is titled TTEST–UNEQUAL, and the question is, "Is there a difference in contribution levels to nonprofits between married and never married females?"

Variable	*Description*
Married Females	Amount of money donated to not-for-profit organizations in dollars per year by married females
Never Married Females	Amount of money donated to not-for-profit organizations in dollars per year by never married females

Using the t-Test: Two-Sample Assuming Unequal Variances Tool

1. **Select the Data Analysis option** from the Data tab.
2. **Double-click** on the **t-Test: Two-Sample Assuming Unequal Variances option** in the Data Analysis dialog box and you will see the t-Test: Two-Sample Assuming Unequal Variances dialog box shown in Figure 38.1.
3. Be sure that the Labels box in the Input area is checked.
4. **Click the RefEdit button** in the Variable 1 Range entry box and select the data you want to use in the analysis. In this example, it is Cells B1 through B21. **Click the RefEdit button again.**
5. **Click the RefEdit button** in the Variable 2 Range entry box and select the data you want to use in the analysis. In this example, it is Cells C1 through C23. **Click the RefEdit button again.**
6. **Click the RefEdit button** and enter the output range. In this example, Cell E1 was selected. **Click the RefEdit button again** and **click OK.**

The Final Output

The results are shown in Figure 38.2 with a t value of –.28, which is not significant beyond the .05 level (as specified in the dialog box you see in Figure 38.1), indicating that there is no difference in the amount of dollars contributed to nonprofit organizations by married and never married females.

Figure 38.1 The t-Test: Two-Sample Assuming Unequal Variances Dialog Box

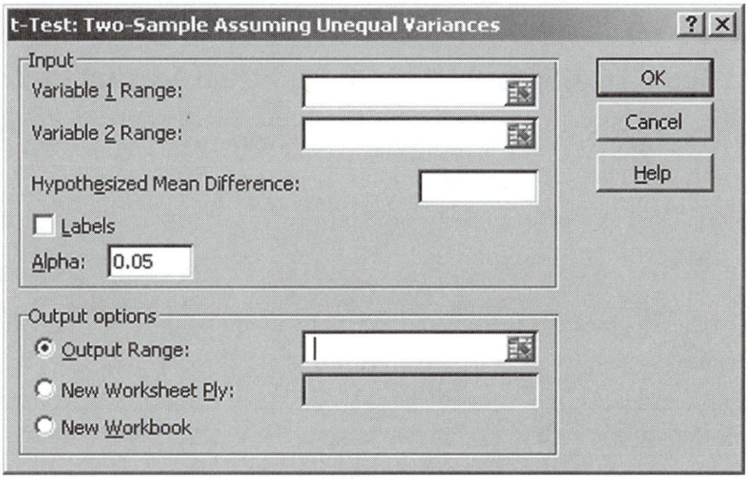

t-Test: Two-Sample Assuming Unequal Variances

Input

Variable 1 Range:

Variable 2 Range:

Hypothesized Mean Difference:

Labels

Alpha: 0.05

Output options

Output Range:

New Worksheet Ply:

New Workbook

OK

Cancel

Help

Figure 38.2 The t-Test: Two-Sample Assuming Unequal Variances Output

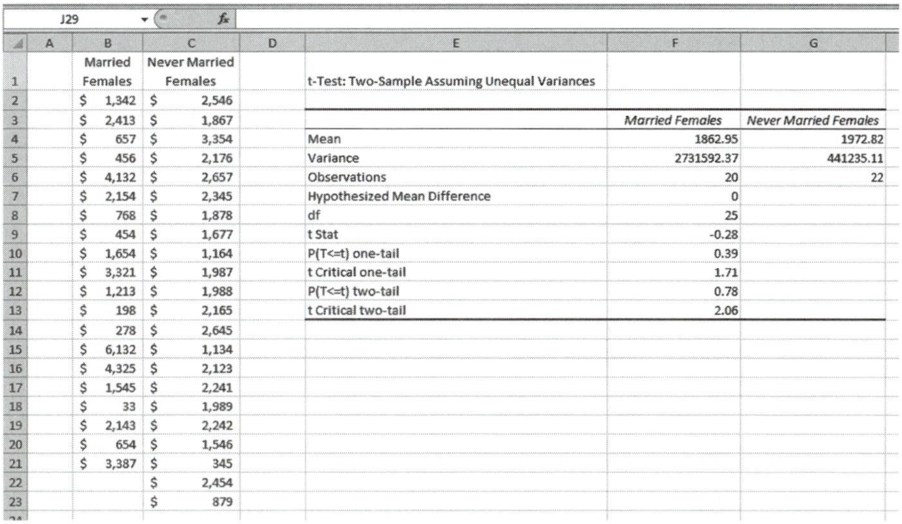

J29

	A	B	C	D	E	F	G
1		Married Females	Never Married Females		t-Test: Two-Sample Assuming Unequal Variances		
2		$ 1,342	$ 2,546				
3		$ 2,413	$ 1,867			*Married Females*	*Never Married Females*
4		$ 657	$ 3,354		Mean	1862.95	1972.82
5		$ 456	$ 2,176		Variance	2731592.37	441235.11
6		$ 4,132	$ 2,657		Observations	20	22
7		$ 2,154	$ 2,345		Hypothesized Mean Difference	0	
8		$ 768	$ 1,878		df	25	
9		$ 454	$ 1,677		t Stat	-0.28	
10		$ 1,654	$ 1,164		P(T<=t) one-tail	0.39	
11		$ 3,321	$ 1,987		t Critical one-tail	1.71	
12		$ 1,213	$ 1,988		P(T<=t) two-tail	0.78	
13		$ 198	$ 2,165		t Critical two-tail	2.06	
14		$ 278	$ 2,645				
15		$ 6,132	$ 1,134				
16		$ 4,325	$ 2,123				
17		$ 1,545	$ 2,241				
18		$ 33	$ 1,989				
19		$ 2,143	$ 2,242				
20		$ 654	$ 1,546				
21		$ 3,387	$ 345				
22			$ 2,454				
23			$ 879				

Excel QuickGuide 39

t-Test: Two-Sample Assuming Equal Variances

What the t-Test: Two-Sample Assuming Equal Variances Tool Does

The t-Test: Two-Sample for Means computes a *t* value between means for two independent measures when the variances for each group are equal.

The Data Set

The data set used in this example is titled TTEST—EQUAL, and the question is, "Is there a difference in weekly sales levels in units sold between Region 1 and Region 2?"

Variable	*Description*
Sales R1	Weekly sales in units for Region 1
Sales R2	Weekly sales in units for Region 2

Using the t-Test: Two-Sample Assuming Equal Variances Tool

1. **Select the Data Analysis option** from the Data tab.
2. **Double-click** on the **t-Test: Two-Sample Assuming Equal Variances** option in the Data Analysis dialog box and you will see the t-Test: Two-Sample Assuming Equal Variances dialog box shown in Figure 39.1.
3. Be sure that the Labels box in the Input area is checked.
4. **Click the RefEdit button** in the Variable 1 Range entry box and select the data you want to use in the analysis. In this example, it is Cells C1 through C17. **Click the RefEdit button.**
5. **Click the RefEdit button** in the Variable 2 Range entry box and select the data you want to use in the analysis. In this example, it is Cells D1 through D17. **Click the RefEdit button.**
6. **Click the RefEdit button** and enter the output range. In this example, Cell F1 was selected. **Click the RefEdit button again** and **click OK.**

The Final Output

The results are shown in Figure 39.2 with a *t* value of –2.76, which is significant beyond the .05 level (as specified in the dialog box you see in Figure 39.1) for a two-tailed test, indicating that there is a difference in sales between the two regions.

Figure 39.1 The t-Test: Two-Sample Assuming Equal Variances Dialog Box

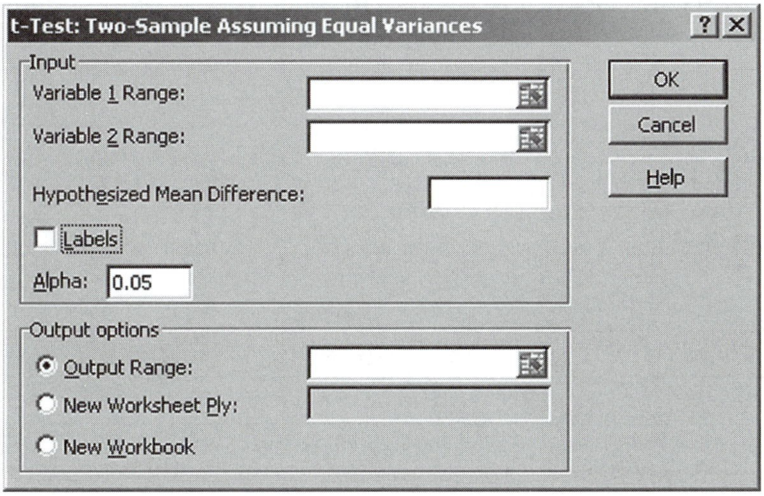

t-Test: Two-Sample Assuming Equal Variances

Input

Variable 1 Range:

Variable 2 Range:

Hypothesized Mean Difference:

Labels

Alpha: 0.05

Output options

Output Range:

New Worksheet Ply:

New Workbook

OK

Cancel

Help

Figure 39.2 The t-Test: Two-Sample Assuming Equal Variances Output

F25

	A	B	C	D	E	F	G	H
1		Week	Sales R1	Sales R2		t-Test: Two-Sample Assuming Equal Variances		
2		1	$ 465	$ 657				
3		2	$ 465	$ 789			*Sales R1*	*Sales R2*
4		3	$ 423	$ 456		Mean	408.563	531.688
5		4	$ 398	$ 655		Variance	3013.063	28745.563
6		5	$ 387	$ 354		Observations	16	16
7		6	$ 416	$ 775		Pooled Variance	15879.313	
8		7	$ 401	$ 726		Hypothesized Mean Difference	0	
9		8	$ 326	$ 389		df	30	
10		9	$ 345	$ 456		t Stat	-2.764	
11		10	$ 476	$ 331		P(T<=t) one-tail	0.005	
12		11	$ 312	$ 412		t Critical one-tail	1.697	
13		12	$ 334	$ 588		P(T<=t) two-tail	0.010	
14		13	$ 431	$ 312		t Critical two-tail	2.042	
15		14	$ 478	$ 331				
16		15	$ 453	$ 589				
17		16	$ 427	$ 687				

Excel QuickGuide 40

Anova: Single Factor

What the Anova: Single Factor Tool Does

The Anova: Single Factor tests for differences between the means of two or more groups.

The Data Set

The data set used in this example is titled Anova—Single Factor, and the question is, "Is there a difference in language proficiency (LP) as a function of number of hours of weekly practice?"

Variable	*Description*
Weekly Practice	No hours, 5 hours, or 10 hours
LP	Language proficiency on a scale from 1 through 20

Using the Anova: Single Factor Tool

1. **Select the Data Analysis option** from the Data tab.
2. **Double-click** on the **Anova: Single Factor option** in the Data Analysis dialog box and you will see the Anova: Single Factor dialog box shown in Figure 40.1.
3. Be sure to check the Labels in First Row box.
4. **Click the RefEdit button** in the Input Range entry box and select the data you want to use in the analysis. In this example, it is Cells B2 through D21. **Click the RefEdit icon.**
5. **Click the RefEdit button** and enter the output range. In this example, Cell F2 was selected. **Click the RefEdit button again** and **click OK.**

The Final Output

The results are shown in Figure 40.2 with language proficiency increasing with more practice and the difference between the means of the three groups being significant beyond the .05 level (precisely = .02966) given an F value of 3.16.

Figure 40.1 The Anova: Single Factor Dialog Box

Anova: Single Factor

Input
- Input Range: [ ]
- Grouped By: (•) Columns ( ) Rows
- [ ] Labels in First Row
- Alpha: 0.05

Output options
- ( ) Output Range: [ ]
- (•) New Worksheet Ply: [ ]
- ( ) New Workbook

OK | Cancel | Help

Figure 40.2 The Anova: Single Factor Output

P30 | f_x

	A	B	C	D	E	F	G	H	I	J	K	L
1		Weekly Practice										
2		No Practice	5 Hours	10 Hours		Anova: Single Factor						
3		7	7	15								
4		11	8	18		SUMMARY						
5		13	9	15		*Groups*	*Count*	*Sum*	*Average*	*Variance*		
6		12	10	11		No Practice	19	202	10.63	16.47		
7		6	12	16		5 Hours	19	225	11.84	13.36		
8		4	15	15		10 Hours	19	266	14	14.33		
9		7	11	9								
10		8	12	10								
11		16	9	12		ANOVA						
12		11	8	8		*Source of Variation*	*SS*	*df*	*MS*	*F*	*P-value*	*F crit*
13		9	10	19		Between Groups	110.6315789	2	55.32	3.76	0.0297	3.17
14		6	7	16		Within Groups	794.9473684	54	14.72			
15		15	15	6								
16		13	14	19		Total	905.5789474	56				
17		11	17	17								
18		11	16	13								
19		7	20	18								
20		16	11	14								
21		19	14	15								

Excel QuickGuide 41

Anova: Two-Factor With Replication

What the Anova: Two-Factor With Replication Tool Does

The ANOVA: Two Factor With Replication tests for differences between the means of two or more dependent groups or measures.

The Data Set

The data set used in this example is titled Anova With Replication, and the question is, "Is there a difference in satisfaction level (SAT) over four training sessions (Training—Quarter 1 or TQ1, etc.) for 20 unemployed men and women undergoing quarterly training?"

Variable	*Description*
Gender	Male or female
TQ	Training score for each quarter
SAT	Level of satisfaction from 1 to 100 for each of four quarters

Using the Anova: Two-Factor With Replication Tool

1. **Select the Data Analysis option** from the Data tab.
2. **Double-click** on the **Anova: Two-Factor With Replication option** in the Data Analysis dialog box and you will see the Anova: Two-Factor With Replication dialog box shown in Figure 41.1.
3. **Click the RefEdit button** in the Input Range entry box and select the data you want to use in the analysis. In this example, it is Cells B2 through F12. Be sure to select variable labels. **Click the RefEdit button.**
4. **Enter the number of rows** in *each* sample. In this case, it is 5.
5. **Click the RefEdit button** and enter the output range. In this example, Cell A14 was selected. **Click the RefEdit button again** and **click OK.**

The Final Output

The results are shown in Figure 41.2 with several different summary statistics for males and females and three *F* ratios testing the main effects of training, gender, and the interaction.

With *F* values of .01 and .95, respectively, for Gender and the Gender × Training interaction, there was no significant outcome. For the main effect of training ($F = 4.98$), there was a significant outcome showing that regardless of gender, training changed over the four-quarter period. An examination of total means showed that there was an increase in level of satisfaction from TQ1 to TQ4, but it was not positive across all quarters.

Figure 41.1 The Anova: Two-Factor With Replication Dialog Box

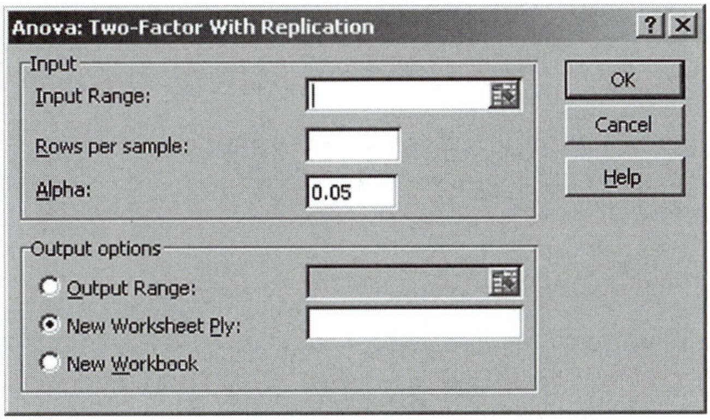

Anova: Two-Factor With Replication

Input
Input Range:
Rows per sample:
Alpha: 0.05

Output options
Output Range:
New Worksheet Ply:
New Workbook

OK
Cancel
Help

Figure 41.2 The Anova: Two-Factor With Replication Output

Anova: Two-Factor With Replication					
SUMMARY	TQ1	TQ2	TQ3	TQ4	Total
Males					
Count	5	5	5	5	20
Sum	320	377	334	374	1405
Average	64.00	75.40	66.80	74.80	70.25
Variance	131.00	188.30	70.20	85.70	125.88
Females					
Count	5	5	5	5	20
Sum	277	361	340	418	1396
Average	55.40	72.20	68.00	83.60	69.80
Variance	161.30	219.20	92.00	186.80	245.85
Total					
Count	10	10	10	10	
Sum	597	738	674	792	
Average	59.70	73.80	67.40	79.20	
Variance	150.46	183.96	72.49	142.62	
ANOVA					
Source of Variation	*SS*	*df*	*MS*	*F*	*P-value*
Sample	2.03	1	2.03	0.01	0.91
Columns	2119.28	3	706.43	4.98	0.01
Interaction	405.67	3	135.22	0.95	0.43
Within	4538.00	32	141.81		
Total	7064.98	39			

Excel QuickGuide 42

Anova: Two-Factor Without Replication

What the Anova: Two-Factor Without Replication Tool Does

The Anova: Two-Factor Without Replication tests for differences between the means of two or more independent groups or measures.

The Data Set

The data set used in this example is titled Anova Without Replication, and the question is, "Does happiness, as measured by the Happy Scale (HS), differ as a function of where people live (residence) and their political affiliation?"

Variable	*Description*
Residence	Rural or urban
Political Affiliation	Party 1 or Party 2
HS	Happiness Scale

Using the Anova: Two-Factor Without Replication Tool

1. **Select the Data Analysis option** from the Data tab.
2. **Double-click** on the **Anova: Two-Factor Without Replication option** in the Data Analysis dialog box and you will see the Anova: Two-Factor Without Replication dialog box shown in Figure 42.1.
3. **Click the RefEdit button** in the Input Range entry box and select the data you want to use in the analysis. In this example, it is Cells B2 through D22. Be sure to check the Labels box. **Click the RefEdit button.**
4. **Click the RefEdit button** and enter the output range. In this example, Cell F1 was selected. **Click the RefEdit button again** and **click OK.**

The Final Output

The (partial) results are shown in Figure 42.2 with the overall *F* values for Political affiliation (.82) not being significant and for Residence (4.41) being significant at the .05 level. There is no test of the interaction, with the final conclusion being that Rural residents (average happiness score of 7.30) are happier than Urban residents (average happiness score of 5.90).

Figure 42.1 The Anova: Two-Factor Without Replication Dialog Box

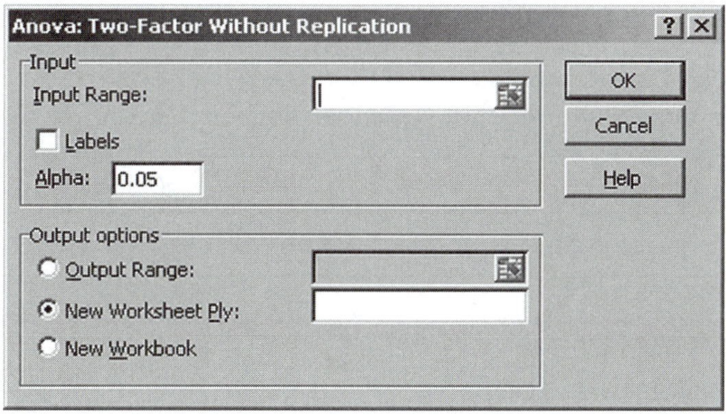

Anova: Two-Factor Without Replication

Input
Input Range:
Labels
Alpha: 0.05

Output options
Output Range:
New Worksheet Ply:
New Workbook

OK
Cancel
Help

Figure 42.2 The Anova: Two-Factor Without Replication (Partial) Output

ANOVA

Source of Variation	*SS*	*df*	*MS*	*F*	*P-value*	*F crit*
Rows	69.6	19	3.66	0.82	0.66	2.17
Columns	19.6	1	19.60	4.41	0.05	4.38
Error	84.4	19	4.44			
Total	173.6	39				

Excel QuickGuide 43

The Correlation Tool

What the Correlation Tool Does

The Correlation tool computes the value of the Pearson product-moment correlation between two variables.

The Data Set

The data set used in this example is titled CORRELATION, and the question is, "What is the correlation between number of years teaching and teaching skills?"

Variable	*Description*
Years Teaching	Number of years teaching
Teaching Skills	Teaching skills rated from 1 to 10

Using the Correlation Tool

1. **Select the Data Analysis option** from the Data tab.
2. **Double-click on the Correlation option** in the Data Analysis dialog box and you will see the Correlation dialog box shown in Figure 43.1.
3. **Click the RefEdit button** in the Input Range entry box and select the data you want to use in the analysis. In this example, it is Cells C1 through D21. Be sure to check the Labels in First Row box. **Click the RefEdit button again.**
4. **Click the RefEdit button** and enter the output range. In this example, Cell F1 is selected. **Click the RefEdit button again** and **click OK.**

The Final Output

The results are shown in Figure 43.2 with the correlation between Years Teaching and Teaching Skills calculated to be .67.

Figure 43.1 The Correlation Dialog Box

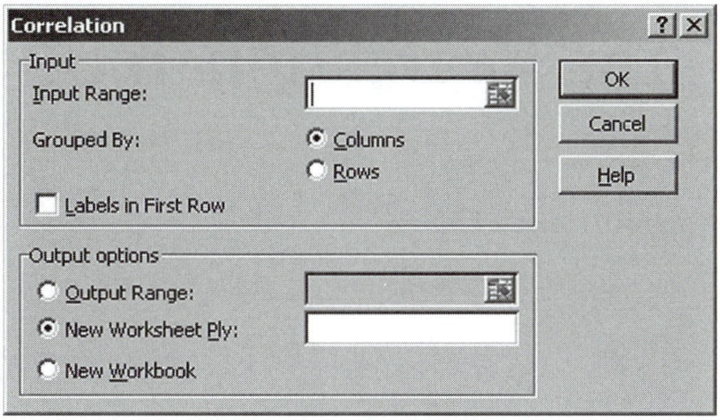

Correlation

Input

Input Range:

Grouped By: Columns / Rows

Labels in First Row

Output options

Output Range:

New Worksheet Ply:

New Workbook

OK

Cancel

Help

Figure 43.2 The Correlation Output

O29

	A	B	C	D	E	F	G	H
1		ID	Years Teaching	Teaching Skills			*Years Teaching*	*Teaching Skills*
2		1	14	8		Years Teaching	1	
3		2	21	10		Teaching Skills	0.67	1
4		3	5	6				
5		4	26	9				
6		5	13	8				
7		6	9	6				
8		7	11	9				
9		8	5	5				
10		9	17	9				
11		10	25	9				
12		11	31	9				
13		12	19	7				
14		13	12	9				
15		14	5	8				
16		15	1	3				
17		16	11	7				
18		17	16	8				
19		18	13	9				
20		19	15	9				
21		20	7	8				

Excel QuickGuide 44

The Regression Tool

What the Regression Tool Does

The Regression tool uses a linear regression model to predict a Y outcome from an X variable.

The Data Set

The data set used in this example is titled REGRESSION, and the question is, "How well does the average number of hours studying predict GPA?"

Variable	*Description*
Hours	Hours studying each week
GPA	Grade point average

Using the Regression Tool

1. **Select the Data Analysis option** from the Data tab.
2. **Double-click on the Regression option** in the Data Analysis dialog box and you will see the Regression dialog box shown in Figure 44.1. Be sure to check the Labels box.
3. **Click the RefEdit button** in the Input Y Range entry box and select the data you want to use in the analysis. In this example, it is Cells C1 through C21. **Click the RefEdit button again.**
4. **Click the RefEdit button** in the Input X Range entry box and select the data you want to use in the analysis. In this example, it is Cells B1 through B21. **Click the RefEdit button again.**
5. **Click the Confidence level box.**
6. **Click the Output Range button, click the RefEdit button,** and enter the output range. In this example, Cell E1 is selected. **Click the RefEdit button again** and **click OK.**

The Final Output

The results in Figure 44.2 show the formula for the regression line to be

$$Y' = .05x + 1.64.$$

Figure 44.1 The Regression Dialog Box

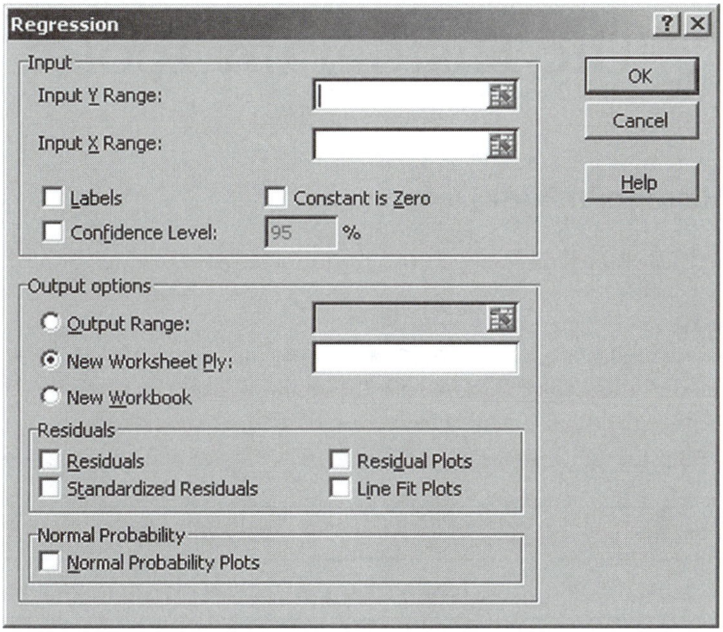

Regression

Input
Input Y Range:
Input X Range:
Labels
Constant is Zero
Confidence Level: 95 %

Output options
Output Range:
New Worksheet Ply:
New Workbook

Residuals
Residuals
Residual Plots
Standardized Residuals
Line Fit Plots

Normal Probability
Normal Probability Plots

OK
Cancel
Help

Figure 44.2 The Regression Output

SUMMARY OUTPUT								
Regression Statistics								
Multiple R	0.50							
R Square	0.25							
Adjusted R Square	0.21							
Standard Error	0.64							
Observations	20							
ANOVA								
	df	*SS*	*MS*	*F*	*Significance F*			
Regression	1	2.55	2.55	6.14	0.02			
Residual	18	7.49	0.42					
Total	19	10.04						
	Coefficients	*Standard Error*	*t Stat*	*P-value*	*Lower 95%*	*Upper 95%*	*Lower 95.0%*	*Upper 95.0%*
Intercept	1.64	0.45	3.63	0.00	0.69	2.59	0.69	2.59
Hours (X)	0.05	0.02	2.48	0.02	0.01	0.10	0.01	0.10

Excel QuickGuide 45

The Histogram Tool

What the Histogram Tool Does

The Histogram tool creates an image of the frequencies of set values organized in classes.

The Data Set

The data set used in this example is titled HISTOGRAM, and the question is, "What is the frequency of first-year, second-year, third-year, and fourth-year students in a sample of 25 students?" The Bin Range represents the categories into which you want to sort data.

Variable	*Description*
Class	1 = 1st year, 2 = 2nd year, 3 = 3rd year, and 4 = 4th year

Using the Histogram Tool

1. **Select the Data Analysis option** from the Data tab.
2. **Double-click on the Histogram option** in the Data Analysis dialog box and you will see the Histogram dialog box shown in Figure 45.1. Be sure to check the Labels box.
3. **Click the RefEdit button** in the Input Range entry box and select the data you want to use in the analysis. In this example, it is Cells B1 through B26. **Click the RefEdit button.**
4. **Click the RefEdit button** in the Bin Range entry box and select the data you want to use in the analysis. In this example, it is Cells C1 through C5. **Click the RefEdit button again.**
5. **Click the Chart Output and Cumulative Percentage boxes.**
6. **Click the Output Range button, click the RefEdit button,** and enter the output range. In this example, Cell E1 is selected. **Click the RefEdit button again** and **click OK.**

The Final Output

The results in Figure 45.2 show the frequency of each value in the bin range plus the cumulative frequency. A histogram of the frequencies as well as a line of the cumulative frequencies are also produced.

Figure 45.1 The Histogram Dialog Box

Histogram

Input

Input Range:

Bin Range:

☑ Labels

Output options

◉ Output Range:

○ New Worksheet Ply:

○ New Workbook

☐ Pareto (sorted histogram)

☐ Cumulative Percentage

☐ Chart Output

OK

Cancel

Help

Figure 45.2 The Histogram Output

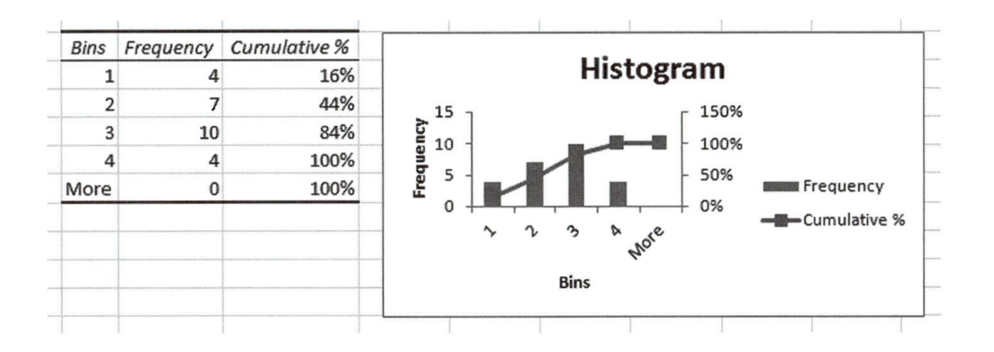

Bins	*Frequency*	*Cumulative %*
1	4	16%
2	7	44%
3	10	84%
4	4	100%
More	0	100%

Index